Healthy Air Fryer Cookbook

250 Easy and Tasty Air Fryer Recipes

for Smart People on a Budget.

by

Henry Wilson

Table of Contents

Introduction

In this book, you will find all the information that you will need to make the most of your Air Fryer. There are also 100 recipes given in this book that will help you to cook healthy and tasty food that you can prepare quickly.

The recipes that have been included in this book can be cooked in an Air Fryer. The recipes have also been segregated into different categories for the convenience of the reader. These tried and tested recipes will help you in whipping up a feast by simply making use of one appliance, the Air Fryer.

Air Fryers don't have to be used simply for cooking fries. You can cook so much more than just that. Different breakfast, lunch and dinner recipes have been provided that make use of poultry, meat, seafood and vegetables for cooking some delicious meals.

Introduction To Air Fryers

An air fryer is a simple device used to cook foods by making use of hot air. It generates hot air and circulates it around the food, which helps to cook it evenly. This air replaces oils and fats, thereby providing nourishing food that is healthy.

Air fryers have now become quite popular owing to their user friendliness and ease of use. They are now a much sought after modern appliance and one of the most popular kitchen appliances to cook up healthy meals.

The air fryer works on a simple principle known as the Maillard reaction. This reaction helps with crisping up the meal while maintaining the nutritional value, without the use of oils that may be detrimental to health.

Air Fryer Benefits

It replaces other cooking appliances

You can use your air fryer instead of your oven, microwave, deep fryer and dehydrator! In a small device, you can quickly prepare perfect dishes for every meal without sacrificing flavor.

It cooks faster than traditional cooking methods

Air frying works by circulating hot air around the cooking chamber. This results in fast, even cooking, using a fraction of the energy in your oven. Most air fryers can be set to a maximum temperature of 400 ° F. For this reason, just about anything you can do in an oven, you can do in an air fryer.

It uses little or no cooking oil

A main selling point of air fryers is that you can achieve beautifully cooked foods with little to no cooking oil. While that may be attractive to some because it can mean lower fat content, people following the keto diet can rejoice because it means fewer calories, which still matter if you're doing keto for weight loss.

Quick cleaning

Regardless of the cooking method used, your stove may soon become dirty, but with the small cooking chamber and the removable basket of your air fryer, deep cleaning is a breeze!

Air Fryer Functions

The Air fryer cooks food quite fast owing to this innovative technology and serves up a hearty meal in no time at all. The fryer can be used to cook in many different ways that are outlined as follows:

Roasting foods

Roasting is one of the main ways to cook using an air fryer. The air fryer cuts the time in half when it comes to roasting foods. It makes use of rapid air technology that is designed to cook foods at a faster pace. The advantage is that you spend less time slaving in front of a hot stove and get it done in even less time than you might expect.

Frying foods

The air fryer is also very useful for frying foods. It helps in frying foods at a faster pace without making them too oily. As a matter of fact, you need not worry about using any oil at all, as it effectively fries foods without it. The fryer makes use of hot air alone to crisp up the foods that you want to fry.

Grilling foods

Most of us dread the thought of grilling foods, as we have to prepare the grill for it and get the temperature right to grill the food properly. However, the job becomes much easier with an air fryer. The temperature is preset and all you have to do is place the ingredients in the fryer. Forget about having to flip the food to cook it on both sides, as the fryer will do the job for you.

Baking foods

Just like grilling, the air fryer also bakes foods. Forget having to rely on the traditional oven to bake your foods as the air fryer does the job in half the time. The air fryer gives you almost the same results as a conventional oven and therefore makes for an excellent choice. The air fryer also comes with a baking attachment intended to bake foods. Just like a regular oven, all you have to do is preheat the air fryer and put your food into it.

Breakfast Recipes

Air Fryer Baked Apples

Preparation Time: 20 minutes | Yield: 2 Servings

Ingredients:

- 1 medium apple or pear
- 2 Tbsp. chopped walnuts
- 1 ½ tsp. light margarine, melted
- ¼ tsp. cinnamon
- ¼ tsp. nutmeg
- ¼ cup water
- 2 Tbsp. raisins

Directions:

Preheat air fryer to 350° F. Cut the apple or pear in half around the middle and spoon out some of the flesh. Place the apple or pear in frying pan (which may be provided with the air fryer) or on the bottom of the air fryer (after removing the accessory). In a small bowl, combine margarine, cinnamon, nutmeg, walnuts and raisins. Spoon this mixture into the centers of the apple/pear halves. Pour water into the pan. Bake for 20 minutes.

Nutritional Information:

Calories: 194, Fat: 2g, Carbs: 23g, Protein: 4g

Air Fryer French Toast

Preparation Time: 10 minutes | Yield: 2 Servings

Ingredients:

- 4 Slices Wholemeal Bread
- 2 Large Eggs
- 1 Tbsp Honey
- 1 Tsp Cinnamon

- ¼ Cup Whole Milk
- ¼ Cup Brown Sugar
- Pinch Of Nutmeg
- Pinch Of Icing Sugar

Directions:

Chop up your slices of bread into soldiers. Each slice should make 4 soldiers. Place the rest of your ingredients (apart from the icing sugar) into a mixing bowl and mix well. Dip each soldier into the mixture so that it is well coated and then place it into the Air Fryer. When you're done you will have 16 soldiers and then should all be nice and wet from the mixture. Place on 160c for 10 minutes or until they are nice and crispy like toast and are no longer wet. Halfway through cooking turn them over so that both sides of the soldiers have a good chance to be evenly cooked. Serve with a sprinkle of icing sugar and some fresh berries.

Nutritional Information:

Calories: 170, Fat: 8g, Carbs: 19g, Protein: 6g

Air Fryer Frittata

Preparation Time: 20 minutes | Yield: 2 Servings

Ingredients:

- 1 cup egg whites
- 2 Tbsp. skim milk
- ¼ cup sliced tomato
- ¼ cup sliced mushrooms
- 2 Tbsp. chopped fresh chives
- Black pepper, to taste

Directions:

Preheat Air Fryer at 320° F. In a bowl, combine all the ingredients. Transfer to a greased frying pan (which may be provided with the air fryer) or to the bottom of the air fryer (after removing the accessory). Bake for 15 minutes or until frittata is cooked through.

Nutritional Information:

Calories: 381, Fat: 24g, Carbs: 2g, Protein: 31g

Air Fryer Puffed Egg Tarts

Preparation Time: 20 minutes | Yield: 4 Servings

Ingredients:

- 1 cup All-purpose flour
- 1 sheet frozen puff pastry half a 17.3-oz/490 g package, thawed
- 4 large eggs
- 3 /4 cup shredded cheese such as Cheddar or Monterey Jack, divided
- 1 tbsp minced fresh parsley or chives optional

Directions:

On a lightly floured surface, unfold pastry sheet. Cut into 4 squares. Preheat air fryer to 390°F (200°C). Place 2 squares in air fryer basket, spacing them apart. Air-fry for 10 minutes or until pastry is light golden brown. Open basket and, using a metal spoon, press down the centers of each square to make an indentation. Sprinkle 3 tbsp (45 mL) cheese into each indentation and carefully crack an egg into the center of each pastry. Air-fry for 7 to 11 minutes or until eggs are cooked to desired doneness. Transfer to a wire rack set over waxed paper and let cool for 5 minutes. Sprinkle with half the parsley, if desired. Serve warm. Repeat steps 3 to 5 with the remaining pastry squares, cheese, eggs and parsley.

Nutritional Information:

Calories: 446, Fat: 21g, Carbs: 27g, Protein: 14g

Air Fryer Hash Browns

Preparation Time: 20 minutes | Yield: 8 Servings

Ingredients:

- Large potatoes - 4 - peeled and finely grated
- Corn flour - 2 tablespoon
- Salt - to taste
- Pepper powder - to taste
- Chili flakes - 2 teaspoon
- Garlic powder - 1 teaspoon (optional)
- Onion Powder - 1 teaspoon (optional)
- Vegetable Oil - 1 + 1 teaspoon

Directions:

Soak the shredded potatoes in cold water. Drain the water. Repeat the step to drain excess starch from potatoes. In a non-stick pan heat 1 teaspoon of vegetable oil and saute shredded potatoes till cooked slightly for 3-4 mins. Cool it down and transfer the potatoes to a plate. Add corn flour, salt, pepper, garlic and onion powder and chili flakes and mix together roughly. Spread over the plate and pat it firmly with your fingers. Regrigerate it for 20 minutes. Preheat air fryer at 180C. Take out the now refrigerated potato and divide into equal pieces with a knife. Brush the wire basket of the air fryer with little oil. Place the hash brown pieces in the basket and fry for 15 minutes at 180C. Take out the basket and flip the hash browns at 6 minutes so that they are air fried uniformly. Serve it hot with ketchup.

Nutritional Information:

Calories: 127, Fat: 2g, Carbs: 27g, Protein: 4g

Air Fryer Bacon

Preparation Time: 10 minutes | Yield: 2 Servings

Ingredients:

- 6 strips of bacon
- 2 Slices of Bread

Directions:

Place the bacon in the bottom of your air fryer basket. I have a 3.5 quart air fryer and was able to get 6 strips of bacon on the bottom. Place the wire rack over your bacon that came with air fryer. This is optional. If you don't have a wire rack that came with your air fryer, then you don't need one. Cook at 350 for 7 to 9 minutes. Open up the air fryer and flip the bacon. Put the air fryer basket back in and cook for another 3 minutes or until however crispy you like your bacon. Put 3 crispy bacon pieces inside 2 bread pieces and enjoy!

Nutritional Information:

Calories: 37, Fat: 3g, Carbs: 1g, Protein: 3g

Air Fryer Omelette

Preparation Time: 10 minutes | Yield: 4 Servings

Ingredients:

- 2 eggs
- 1/4 cup milk
- Pinch of salt
- 1/4 cup shredded cheese

- Fresh meat and vegetables, diced (use red bell pepper, green onions, ham and mushrooms)
- 1 teaspoon McCormick Breakfast Seasoning

Directions:

In a small bowl, mix the eggs and milk until well combined. Add a pinch of salt to the egg mixture. Add your vegetables to the egg mixture. Pour the egg mixture into a well-greased 6"x3" pan. Place the pan into the basket of the air fryer. Cook at 350F Fahrenheit for 8-10 minutes. Halfway through cooking sprinkle the breakfast seasoning onto the eggs and sprinkle the cheese over the top. Use a thin spatula to loosen the omelette from the sides of the pan and transfer to a plate. Garnish with extra green onions, optional

Nutritional Information:

Calories: 274, Fat: 20g, Carbs: 6g, Protein: 13g

Air Fryer Breakfast Pockets

Preparation Time: 10 minutes | Yield: 4 Servings

Ingredients:

- one box puff pastry sheets
- 5 eggs
- 1/2 cup sausage crumbled, cooked

- 1/2 cup bacon, cooked
- 1/2 cup cheddar cheese, shredded

Directions:

Cook eggs as regular scrambled eggs. Add meat to the egg mixture while you cook, if desired. Spread out puff pastry sheets on a cutting board and cut out rectangles with a cookie cutter or knife, making sure they are all uniform so they will fit nicely together. Spoon preferred egg, meat, and cheese combos onto half of the pastry rectangles. Place a pastry rectangle on top of the mixture and press edges together with a fork to seal. Spray with spray oil if you desired a shiny, smooth pastry, but it really is optional. Place breakfast pockets in the air fryer basket and cook for 8-10 minutes at 370 degrees. Watch carefully and check every 2-3 minutes for desired crispness.

Nutritional Information:

Calories: 351, Fat: 8g, Carbs: 41g, Protein: 25g

Flourless Broccoli Quiche

Preparation Time: 20 minutes | Yield: 2 Servings

Ingredients:

- 1 Large Broccoli
- 3 Large Carrots
- 1 Large Tomato
- 100 g Cheddar Cheese grated
- 20 g Feta Cheese

- 150 ml Whole Milk
- 2 Large Eggs
- 1 Tsp Parsley
- 1 Tsp Thyme
- Salt & Pepper

Directions:

Chop up your broccoli into florets. Peel and dice your carrots. Place your carrots and broccoli into a food steamer and cook for 20 minutes or until soft. In a measuring jug add all your seasonings. Crack the eggs into the jug and mix well. Add the milk a bit at a time until you have a pale mixture. When the steamer has finished drain the vegetables and line the bottom of your quiche dish with them. Layer with the tomatoes and then add your cheese on top. Pour the liquid over and then add a little bit more cheese on top. Place in the air fryer and cook for 20 minutes on 180c. Serve.

Nutritional Information:

Calories: 340, Fat: 24g, Carbs: 22g, Protein: 9g

Breakfast Style Air Fryer Potatoes

Preparation Time: 20 minutes | Yield: 4 Servings

Ingredients:

- 2 medium sized Russet potatoes ~13 ounces total or roughly 2 generous cups, chopped in roughly one inch pieces
- Few generous spritzes oil spray
- Pinch salt & pepper
- 1 small bell pepper ~ 5 ounces or roughly 3/4 cup, chopped medium
- 1 small onion ~ 4 ounces or roughly 3/4 cup, chopped medium

Directions:

Put potatoes into air fryer basket. Spritz with oil spray, shake, spritz again, and add a pinch of salt. Set the air fryer to 400 degrees and ten minutes. Stop once to shake during cooking time. (Feel free to stir, if the potatoes aren't moving around enough.) After the potatoes have cooked for ten minutes, add the bell pepper and onions. Add another spritz of oil, and shake basket. Set the air fryer to 400 degrees and 15 minutes. During the last 5 minutes of cooking, check on the potatoes to make sure they aren't getting too brown. Depending on the size of your potatoes, you may need slightly less or slightly more time. If needed, add a few more minutes to the cooking time. Add salt to taste and serve.

Nutritional Information:

Calories: 21, Fat: 1g, Carbs: 17g, Protein: 3g

Keto Breakfast Recipes

Breakfast Egg Rolls

Preparation Time: 10 minutes │ Yield: 4 Servings

Ingredients:

- 1 tsp minced ginger
- 4 ½ cups packaged coleslaw mix (shredded cabbage and carrots)
- 3 medium cooked scallions
- 3 Tbsp low sodium soy sauce
- 1 ½ tsp sesame oil
- 1 pound uncooked ground chicken breast (can sub ground pork, turkey, or turkey sausage)
- 1 16 oz package of Egg Roll Wrappers (I only used 8 of them)
- 1 egg

Directions:

Brown the sausage/meat in a medium non-stick skillet until cooked all the way through and then add the ginger. Add soy sauce and sesame oil. Add full bag of coleslaw, stir until coated with sauce. Add chopped scallions, mix thoroughly and cook on medium high heat until the coleslaw has reduced by half. Set the egg roll mixture aside. Lay egg roll wrap in front of you so that it looks like a diamond. Place 3 tablespoons of filling in center of egg roll wrapper. Brush each edge with egg wash. Fold bottom point up over filling and roll once. Fold in right and left points. Finish rolling. Set aside and repeat with remaining filling. Heat Air Fryer to (370°F). Set your stuffed egg rolls on the bottom of the air fryer basket and fry for 7 minutes or until they are golden brown.

Nutritional Information:

Calories: 181, Fat: 4g, Carbs: 18G, Protein: 8g

Keto Air Fryer Fish Sticks

Preparation Time: 20 minutes │ Yield: 2 Servings

Ingredients:

- 1 lb white fish such as cod
- 1/4 cup mayonnaise
- 2 tbsp Dijon mustard
- 2 tbsp water
- 1 1/2 cups pork rind panko such as Pork King Good
- 3/4 tsp cajun seasoning
- Salt and pepper to taste

Directions:

Spray the air fryer rack with non-stick cooking spray (I use avocado oil spray). Pat the fish dry and cut into sticks about 1 inch by 2 inches wide (how you are able to cut it will depend a little on what kind of fish you by and how thick and wide it is). In a small shallow bowl, whisk together the mayo, mustard, and water. In another shallow bowl, whisk together the pork rinds and Cajun seasoning. Add salt and pepper to taste (both the pork rinds and seasoning could have a fair bit of salt so dip a finger in to taste how salty it is). Working with one piece of fish at a time, dip into the mayo mixture to coat and then tap off the excess. Dip into the pork rind mixture and toss to coat. Place on the air fryer rack. Set to Air Fry at 400F and bake 5 minutes, the flip the fish sticks with tongs and bake another 5 minutes. Serve immediately.

Nutritional Information:

Calories: 263, Fat: 16G, Carbs: 1G, Protein: 26g

Low Carb Mozzarella Sticks

Preparation Time: 15 minutes | Yield: 2 Servings

Ingredients:

- 12 Mozzarella sticks string cheese, cut in half
- 2 large Eggs beaten
- 1/2 cup Almond flour
- 1/2 cup Parmesan cheese the powdered kind
- 1 teaspoon Italian seasoning
- 1/2 teaspoon Garlic Salt

Directions:

In a bowl combine almond flour, Parmesan cheese, Italian seasoning, and garlic salt. In a separate bowl whisk eggs. One at a time coat your mozzarella stick halves in egg and then toss in the coating mixture. As you finish place them in a resealable container. If you have to make more than 1 layer place parchment paper between the layers of mozzarella sticks. Freeze mozzarella sticks for 30 minutes. Remove from freezer and place in Philips AirFryer. Set to 400 degrees F and cook for 5 minutes. Open air fryer and let stand for 1 minute before moving low carb mozzarella sticks to a plate.

Nutritional Information:

Calories: 382, Fat: 27G, Carbs: 1G, Protein: 31g

Homemade Sausage Rolls

Preparation Time: 25 minutes | Yield: 4 Servings

Ingredients:

- 225 g Almond Flour
- 100 g Butter
- 1 Tbsp Olive Oil
- 300 g Sausage Meat
- 1 Medium Egg beaten
- 1 Tsp Mustard
- 1 Tsp Parsley
- Salt & Pepper

Directions:

Start by making your pastry. Place the flour, the seasoning and the butter into a mixing bowl and using the rubbing in method, rub the fat into the flour until you have a mixture that resembles bread crumbs. Add the olive oil and a little water (a bit at a time) and using your hands make the mixture into a flaky dough. Knead the pastry as you mix it together so that it becomes lovely and smooth. Roll out the pastry onto a worktop and create a square shape of pastry. Using a teaspoon (or your fingers) rub the mustard into the pastry. Place the sausage meat in the centre and brush the edges of the pastry with egg. Roll up the sausage rolls and then divide into portions. Brush the tops and sides of the sausage rolls with more eggs. Slash the top of the sausage rolls with a knife so that they have the chance to breathe. Cook in the Air fryer at 160C for 20 minutes and then for a further 5 minutes at 200c so that you can have that lovely crunchy pastry. Serve.

Nutritional Information:

Calories: 545, Fat: 45g, Carbs: 25G, Protein: 18g

Easy Air Fryer Omelette

Preparation Time: 15 minutes | Yield: 2 Servings

Ingredients:

- 2 eggs
- 1/4 cup milk
- Pinch of salt
- Fresh meat and vegetables, diced (I used red bell pepper, green onions, ham and mushrooms)
- 1 teaspoon McCormick Good Morning Breakfast Seasoning – Garden Herb
- 1/4 cup shredded cheese (I used cheddar and mozzarella)

Directions:

In a small bowl, mix the eggs and milk until well combined. Add a pinch of salt to the egg mixture. Add your vegetables to the egg mixture. Pour the egg mixture into a well-greased 6"x3" pan. Place the pan into the basket of the air fryer. Cook at 350F Fahrenheit for 8-10 minutes. Halfway through cooking sprinkle the breakfast seasoning onto the eggs and sprinkle the cheese over the top. Use a thin spatula to loosen the omelette from the sides of the pan and transfer to a plate. Garnish with extra green onions, optional

Nutritional Information:

Calories: 274, Fat: 20G, Carbs: 3g, Protein: 16g

Air Fryer Tofu Scramble

Preparation Time: 30 minutes | Yield: 3 Servings

Ingredients:

- 1 block tofu - chopped into 1" pieces
- 2 tablespoons soy sauce
- 1 tablespoon olive oil
- 1 teaspoon turmeric
- 1/2 teaspoon garlic powder
- 1/2 teaspoon onion powder
- 1/2 cup chopped onion
- 1 tablespoon olive oil
- 4 cups broccoli florets

Directions:

In a medium sized bowl, toss together the tofu, soy sauce, olive oil, turmeric, garlic powder, onion powder, and onion. Set aside to marinate. Add the tofu, reserving any leftover marinade. Set the tofu to cook at 370 for 15 minutes, and start the air fryer. While the tofu is cooking, toss the broccoli in the reserved marinade. If there isn't enough to get it all over the broccoli, add a little bit of extra soy sauce. Be careful not to let the broccoli dry out. When there are 5 minutes of cooking time remaining, add the broccoli to the air fryer.

Nutritional Information:

Calories: 150, Fat: 5g, Carbs: 5g, Protein: 10g

Air Fryer Hard Boiled Eggs

Preparation Time: 15 minutes | Yield: 6 Servings

Ingredients:

- 6 eggs

Directions:

Place the eggs onto the air fryer rack giving the eggs enough room so the air will circulate around the egg. Cook the eggs in the air fryer for 15 minutes at 260 degrees F. Remove the eggs and place the eggs into an ice water bath for 10 minutes.

Notes: Never skip the water bath, it helps stop the cooking process and also makes them easier to peel.

Nutritional Information:

Calories: 26, Fat: 4g, Carbs: 0g, Protein: 5g

Fried Cheesecake Bites

Preparation Time: 25 minutes | Yield: 4 Servings

Ingredients:

- 8 ounces cream cheese
- 1/2 cup erythritol
- 2 Tablespoons cream, divided
- 1/2 teaspoon vanilla extract
- 1/2 cup almond flour
- 2 Tablespoons erythritol

Directions

Allow the cream cheese to sit on the counter for 20 minutes to soften. Fit a stand mixer with paddle attachment. Mix the softened cream cheese, 1/2 cup erithrytol, vanilla and 2 Tablespoons heavy cream until smooth. Scoop onto a parchment paper lined baking sheet. Freeze for about 30 minutes, until firm. Mix the almond flour with the 2 Tablespoons erythritol in a small mixing bowl. Dip the frozen cheesecake bites into 2 Tablespoons cream, then roll into the almond flour mixture. Place in an air fryer set at 350, for 5 minutes. Alternatively, you can bake them in the oven for 8 minutes to achieve that crispy outside coating.

Nutritional Information

Calories: 80, Fat: 7g, Carbs: 2G, Protein: 2G

Air Fryer Fried Parmesan Zucchini

Preparation Time: 30 minutes | Yield: 6 Servings

Ingredients

• 2 medium zucchini • 1 large egg • 1/2 cup grated parmesan cheese • 1/4 almond flour	• 1/2 teaspoon garlic powder • 1 teaspoon Italian seasoning • avocado oil spray or other cooking oil spray

Directions:

Slice zucchini into 1/4 to 1/3 of an inch slices. Beat egg well in a separate bowl. Combine grated parmesan cheese, almond flour, garlic powder and Italian seasoning in another bowl. Dip zucchini slice in egg then dip it in the parmesan cheese mixture. Set on parchment lined air fryer tray. Repeat until air fryer tray is full. Lightly spray coated zucchini with avocado oil spray. Set air fryer to 370F for 8 minutes. Remove tray and flip zucchini slices. Spray with avocado oil and cook for another 8 minutes. Repeat process with second batch of zucchini. Serve warm.

Nutritional Information:

Calories: 92, Fat: 5g, Carbs: 4g, Protein: 6g

Keto Creamed Spinach

Preparation Time: 15 minutes | Yield: 2 Servings

Ingredients:

- 1 10 ounce package frozen spinach thawed
- 1/2 cup chopped onion
- 2 teaspoons minced garlic
- 4 ounces cream cheese diced
- 1 teaspoon pepper
- 1 teaspoon salt
- 1/2 teaspoon ground nutmeg
- 1/4 cup shredded Parmesan cheese

Directions:

Grease a 6 inch pan and set aside. In the medium bowl, combine spinach, onion, garlic, cream cheese dices, salt, pepper, and nutmeg. Pour into greased pan. Set air fryer to 350°F for 10 minutes. Open and stir the spinach to mix the cream cheese through the spinach. Sprinkle the Parmesan cheese on top. Set air fryer to 400°F for 5 minutes or until the cheese has melted and browned.

Nutritional Information:

Calories: 273, Fat: 23G, Carbs: 8g, Protein: 8g

Lunch Recipes

Healthy Fish Finger Sandwich

Preparation Time: 20 minutes | Yield: 4 Servings

Ingredients:

- 4 small cod fillets (skin removed)
- salt and pepper
- 2 tbsp flour
- 40g dried breadcrumbs
- spray oil

- 250g frozen peas
- 1 tbsp creme fraiche or greek yogurt
- 10-12 capers
- squeeze of lemon juice
- 4 bread rolls or 8 small slices of bread

Directions:

Pre-heat the Air Fryer. Take each of the cod fillets, season with salt and pepper and lightly dust in the flour. Then roll quickly in the breadcrumbs. The idea is to get a light coating of breadcrumbs on the fish rather than a thick layer. Repeat with each cod fillet. Add a few sprays of oil spray to the bottom of the fryer basket. Place the cod fillets on top and cook on the fish setting (200c) for 15 mins. Whilst the fish is cooking, cook the peas in boiling water for a couple of minutes on the hob or in the microwave. Drain and then add to a blender with the creme fraiche, capers and lemon juice to taste. Blitz until combined. Once the fish has cooked, remove it from the HealthyFry Air Fryer and start layering your sandwich with the bread, fish and pea puree. You can also add lettuce, tartar sauce and any other of your favourite toppings!

Nutritional Information:

Calories: 504, Fat: 17g, Carbs: 67g, Protein: 20g

Chicken Quesadillas

Preparation Time: 20 minutes | Yield: 4 Servings

Ingredients:

- 2 Soft Taco Shells
- Chicken Fajita Strips
- 1/2 cup sliced green peppers
- 1/2 cup sliced
- Shredded Mexican Cheese
- Salsa (optional)
- Sour Cream (optional)

Directions:

Preheat Air Fryer on 370 degrees for about 3 minutes. Spray pan lightly with vegetable oil. Place 1 soft taco shell in pan. Place shredded cheese on shell. (you can use as much or as little as you'd like.) Lay out fajita chicken strips so they are in a single layer. Put your onions and green peppers on top of your chicken. Add more shredded cheese. Place another soft taco shell on top and spray lightly with vegetable oil. Set timer for 4 minutes. Flip over carefully with large spatula. Spray lightly with vegetable oil and place rack on top of shell to hold it in place. Set timer for 4 minutes. If it's not crispy enough for you, leave in for a couple of extra minutes. Remove and cut into 4 slices or 6 slices. Serve with salsa and sour cream if desired.

Nutritional Information:

Calories: 267, Fat: 13g, Carbs: 23g, Protein: 15g

6 Minute Pita Bread Cheese Pizza

Preparation Time: 6 minutes | Yield: 2 Servings

Ingredients:

- 1 Pita Bread
- 1 Tablespoon Pizza Sauce
- 1/4 cup Mozarella Cheese
- 1 drizzle Extra Virgin Olive Oil
- 1 Stainless Steel Short Legged Trivet

Toppings:

- 7 slices Pepperoni or more
- 1/4 cup Sausage
- 1 Tablespoon Yellow/Brown Onion sliced thin
- 1/2 teaspoon Fresh Garlic minced

Directions:

Use a spoon and swirl Pizza Sauce on to Pita Bread. Add your favorite toppings and Cheese. Add a little drizzle of Extra Virgin Olive Oil over top of Pizza. Place in Air Fryer and place a Trivet over Pita Bread. Cook at 350 degrees for 6 minutes. Carefully remove from Air Fryer and cut.

Nutritional Information:

Calories: 324, Fat: 9g, Carbs: 40g, Protein: 20g

Simple Cheese Sandwich

Preparation Time: 8 minutes | Yield: 1 Serving

Ingredients:

- 2 slices Sandwich Bread
- 2-3 slices Cheddar Cheese

- 2 teaspoons Butter or Mayonnaise

Directions:

Place cheese between bread slices and butter the outside of both slices of bread. Place in air fryer and cook at 370 degrees for 8 minutes. Flip, halfway through.

Nutritional Information:

Calories: 430, Fat: 17g, Carbs: 25g, Protein: 18g

Air Fryer Hot Dogs

Preparation Time: 10 minutes | Yield: 2 Servings

Ingredients:

- 2 hot dogs
- 2 hot dog buns

- 2 tablespoons of grated cheese if desired

Directions:

Preheat your air fryer to 390 degrees for about 4 minutes. Place two hot dogs into the air fryer, cook for about 5 minutes. Remove the hot dog from air fryer. Place the hot dog on a bun, add cheese if desired. Place dressed hot dog into the air fryer, and cook for an additional 2 minutes.

Nutritional Information:

Calories: 288, Fat: 13g, Carbs: 23g, Protein: 12g

Bourbon Bacon Burger

Preparation Time: 30 minutes | Yield: 4 Servings

Ingredients:

- 1 tablespoon bourbon
- 2 tablespoons brown sugar
- 3 strips maple bacon, cut in half
- ¾ pound ground beef (80% lean)
- 1 tablespoon minced onion
- 2 tablespoons BBQ sauce
- ½ teaspoon salt
- 2 slices Colby Jack cheese (or Monterey Jack)

- 2 Kaiser rolls
- lettuce and tomato, for serving
- Zesty Burger Sauce:
- 2 tablespoons BBQ sauce
- 2 tablespoons mayonnaise
- ¼ teaspoon ground paprika
- freshly ground black pepper
- freshly ground black pepper

Directions:

Pre-heat the air fryer to 390°F and pour a little water into the bottom of the air fryer drawer. (This will help prevent the grease that drips into the bottom drawer from burning and smoking.) Combine the bourbon and brown sugar in a small bowl. Place the bacon strips in the air fryer basket and brush with the brown sugar mixture. Air-fry at 390F for 4 minutes. Flip the bacon over, brush with more brown sugar and air-fry at 390F for an additional 4 minutes until crispy. While the bacon is cooking, make the burger patties. Combine the ground beef, onion, BBQ sauce, salt and pepper in a large bowl. Mix together thoroughly with your hands and shape the meat into 2 patties. Transfer the burger patties to the air fryer basket and air-fry the burgers at 370°F for 15 to 20 minutes, depending on how you like your burger cooked (15 minutes for rare to medium-rare; 20 minutes for well-done). Flip the burgers over halfway through the cooking process. While the burgers are air-frying, make the burger sauce by combining the BBQ sauce, mayonnaise, paprika and freshly ground black pepper to taste in a bowl. When the burgers are cooked to your liking, top each patty with a slice of Jack cheese and air-fry for an additional minute, just to melt the cheese. Spread the sauce on the inside of the Kaiser rolls, place the burgers on the rolls, top with the bourbon bacon, lettuce and tomato and enjoy!

Nutritional Information:

Calories: 1060, Fat: 65g, Carbs: 77g, Protein: 45g

Leftover Turkey & Cheese Calzone

Preparation Time: 10 minutes | Yield: 4 Servings

Ingredients:

<u>Pizza Dough</u>

- 600 g Plain Flour
- 7 g Yeast easy blend
- 50 ml Warm Milk

- 325 ml Warm Water
- 25 ml Olive Oil
- Salt & Pepper

<u>Main</u>

- 4 Tbsp Homemade Tomato Sauce
- Leftover Turkey brown meat shredded
- 100 g Cheddar Cheese
- 25 g Mozzarella Cheese grated
- 25 g Back Bacon diced

- 1 Large Egg beaten
- 1 Tbsp Tomato Puree
- 1 Tsp Oregano
- 1 Tsp Basil
- 1 Tsp Thyme
- Salt & Pepper

Directions:

<u>Making the dough</u> – mix the flour, yeast and salt together in a large mixing bowl and stir in the olive oil and milk. Gradually add the water, mixing well to form a soft dough. Turn the dough onto a floured workspace and knead for about five minutes, until smooth and elastic. Transfer to a clean bowl, cover with a damp tea towel and leave to rise for 90 minutes or until it has doubled in size. Knead it and repeat the process again so that it has doubled in size again. Roll out your dough and it is ready for its toppings! Preheat your Air Fryer to 180c. Start by rolling out your pizza dough so that they are the size of small pizzas. In a small mixing bowl add together all the seasonings as well as the tomato sauce and puree. Using a cooking brush add a layer of tomato sauce to your pizza bases making sure that it doesn't actually touch the edge with a 1cm space. Layer up your pizza with your turkey, bacon and cheese to one side. With the 1cm gap around your pizza base and using your cooking brush again, brush with beaten egg. Fold your pizza base over so that it resembles an uncooked Cornish pasty and all area that is now visible of the pizza dough to be brushed with more egg. Place in the Air Fryer for 10 minutes at 180c. Serve.

Nutritional Information:

Calories: 158, Fat: 11g, Carbs: 2g, Protein: 10g

Air Fryer Chick-fil-A Nuggets

Preparation Time: 20 minutes | Yield: 6 Servings

Ingredients:

- 1 cup dill pickle juice
- 1 lb boneless skinless chicken breasts, cut into pieces about 1 inch in size
- 1 egg
- 1 cup milk
- 1½ cups flour
- 3 tbsp powdered sugar
- 2 tsp salt
- 1½ tsp pepper
- ½ tsp paprika
- Olive oil spritz

Directions:

Add chicken chunks to pickle juice and marinate in the refrigerator for about 30 minutes. Whisk milk and egg together and set aside. Combine the dry ingredients and stir, then set aside. Preheat air fryer to 370. Remove the chicken from refrigerator, drain and place each into the dry mixture, to the liquid mixture and back to the dry making sure it is well coated, making sure to shake off excess. Cook in a single layer of chicken for 8 minutes or until golden brown, flipping and spritzing with olive oil at the halfway mark. Serve with your favorite dipping sauce

Nutritional Information:

Calories: 256, Fat: 5g, Carbs: 29g, Protein: 22g

Air Fried Chicken Tenders

Preparation Time: 20 minutes | Yield: 2 Servings

Ingredients:

- 12oz of Chicken Breasts
- 35g Panko Bread Crumbs

- 1 Egg White
- 1/8 Cup Flour
- Salt and Pepper

Directions:

Trim chicken breast of any excess fat and cut into tenders. Season each side with salt and pepper. Dip chicken tenders into flour, then egg whites, then panko bread crumbs. Load into air fryer basket and spray with olive spray. Cook at 350 degrees for about 10 minutes or until cooked through

Nutritional Information:

Calories: 375, Fat: 6g, Carbs: 18g, Protein: 57g

Roast Chicken

Preparation Time: 20 minutes | Yield: 4 Servings

Ingredients:

- 4.25 pound whole chicken

Dry rub seasonings

- 3/4 cup kosher salt
- 1/4 cup paprika
- 1/4 cup onion powder
- 1/4 cup garlic powder
- 1/4 cup italian seasoning
- 2 tablespoons dried thyme
- 2 tablespoons dry mustard
- 2 tablespoons cayenne pepper
- 2 tablespoons garlic pepper
- 1/4 cup brown sugar

Directions:

Clean chicken and pat dry. Sprinkle generously with dry rub seasonings above. Spray fry basket with cooking spray and place chicken into the basket with the legs facing down. Roast chicken for 330 degrees Fahrenheit for 30 minutes. Flip chicken. Roast for 20 more minutes at 330 degrees Fahrenheit or until internal temperature of chicken is 165 degrees Fahrenheit.

Nutritional Information:

Calories: 311, Fat: 20g, Carbs: 8g, Protein: 29g

Keto Lunch Recipes

Air Fried Cauliflower Recipe with Sriracha

Preparation Time: 25 minutes | Yield: 4 Servings

Ingredients:

- 1 small head of cauliflower (about 1 1/2 lbs. - 680g), cut into bite sized pieces
- 2 Tablespoons olive oil
- 1 teaspoon sesame oil
- 1 Tablespoon soy sauce
- 1 Tablespoon rice vinegar
- 2 Tablespoons sriracha or any hot sauce

Directions:

In a large bowl combine olive oil, sesame oil, soy sauce, rice vinegar and sriracha hot sauce. Add cauliflower and toss with the marinade. Keep stirring the cauliflower so that it completely soaks up all the marinade (there shouldn't be any marinade pooling at the bottom of the bowl still). Pour cauliflower into air fryer basket and spread evenly in the basket. Air Fry 360°F for 15-20 minutes, shake or gently turn half way. Serve warm and enjoy.

Nutritional Information:

Calories: 155, Fat: 11G, Carbs: 10G, Protein: 5g

Keto Air Fryer Double Cheeseburger

Preparation Time: 15 minutes | Yield: 4 Servings

Ingredients:

- 1/2 lb ground beef (or two pre-made beef patties)
- 2 slices cheese of choice
- 1 pinch pink Himalayan salt
- 1 pinch fresh ground black pepper
- 1 pinch onion powder

Directions:

Form two 1/4 pound hamburger patties (if not using pre-made ones). Lightly salt, pepper, and onion powder the hamburger patties. Place into your air fryer and set to 370°F for 12 minutes. At the 6 minute mark, flip the hamburgers. When the air fryer finishes, place the cheese onto the hamburger patties and shut the drawer for one minute. Remove the patties, stack, and devour!

Nutritional Information:

Calories: 670, Fat: 50g, Carbs: 0g, Protein: 39g

Air Fryer Pork Chops & Broccoli

Preparation Time: 15 minutes | Yield: 4 Servings

Ingredients:

- 2 5 ounce bone-in pork chops
- 2 tablespoons avocado oil, divided
- 1/2 teaspoon paprika
- 1/2 teaspoon onion powder
- 1/2 teaspoon garlic powder
- 1 teaspoon salt, divided
- 2 cups broccoli florets
- 2 cloves garlic, minced

Directions:

Preheat air fryer to 350 degrees. Spray basket with non-stick spray. Drizzle 1 tablespoon of oil both sides of the pork chops. Season the pork chops on both sides with the paprika, onion powder, garlic powder, and 1/2 teaspoon of salt. Place pork chops in the air fryer basket and cook for 5 minutes. While pork chops are cooking, add the broccoli, garlic, remaining 1/2 teaspoon of salt, and remaining tablespoon of oil to a bowl and toss to coat. Open the air fryer and carefully flip the pork chops. Add the broccoli to the basket and return to the air fryer. Cook for 5 more minutes, stirring the broccoli halfway through. Carefully remove the food from the air fryer and serve.

Nutritional Information:

Calories: 283, Fat: 30g, Carbs: 12G, Protein: 40g

Air Fryer Tuna Patties

Preparation Time: 15 minutes | Yield: 4 Servings

Ingredients:

- 2 cans tuna packed in water
- 1 and 1/2 tablespoon almond flour
- 1 and 1/2 tablespoons mayo
- 1 teaspoon dried dill
- 1 teaspoon garlic powder
- 1/2 teaspoon onion powder
- Pinch of salt and pepper
- Juice of 1/2 lemon

Directions:

Combine all ingredients in a bowl and mix well. Tuna should be still wet, but able to form into patties – add an additional tablespoon of almond flour if it's not dry enough to form. Form into 4 patties. Heat to 400 degrees F. Place patties in a single layer in the basket and cook for 10 minutes. Add an additional 3 minutes if you'd like them crispier

Nutritional Information:

Calories: 130, Fat: 4g, Carbs: 5g, Protein: 15g

Air Fryer Carne Asada

Preparation Time: 10 minutes | Yield: 4 Servings

Ingredients:

- 2 medium limes juiced
- 1 medium orange peeled and seeded
- 1 cup cilantro
- 1 jalapeno diced
- 2 tablespoons vegetable oil
- 2 tablespoons vinegar
- 2 teaspoons ancho chile powder
- 1 teaspoons splenda or 2 teaspoon sugar
- 1 teaspoon salt
- 1 teaspoon cumin seeds
- 1 teaspoon coriander seeds
- 1.5 pounds skirt steak

Directions:

Place all ingredients except the skirt steak into a blender and mix until you get a smooth sauce. Cut the skirt steak into four pieces and place into a zip-top plastic bag. Pour the marinade on the steak and let the meat marinate for 30 minutes, or for up to 24 hours in the refrigerator. Set your air fryer to 400F and place the steaks into the air fryer basket. Depending on the size of your air fryer you may have to do this in two batches. Cook for 8 minutes, or until your steak has reached an internal temperature of 145F. It is critical to not overcook skirt steak, so as to not toughen the meat. Let the steak rest for 10 minutes. Don't rush this stage. Slice the steak against the grain (this part is important) and serve.

Nutritional Information:

Calories: 330, Fat: 19G, Carbs: 1G, Protein: 37g

Healthy Eggplant Parmesan

Preparation Time: 25 minutes | Yield: 4 Servings

Ingredients:

- 1 large eggplant mine was around 1.25 lb
- 1/2 cups pork rind panko such as Pork King Good
- 3 tbsp finely grated parmesan cheese
- salt to taste
- 1 tsp Italian seasoning mix
- 3 tbsp whole wheat flour
- 1 egg + 1 tbsp water
- olive oil spray
- 1 cup sugar free marinara sauce
- 1/4 cup grated mozzarella cheese
- fresh parsley or basil to garnish

Directions:

Cut eggplant into roughly 1/2" slices. Rub some salt on both sides of the slices and leave it for at least 10-15 mins. Meanwhile in a small bowl mix egg with water and flour to prepare the batter. In a medium shallow plate combine pork rind panko, parmesan cheese, Italian seasoning blend, and some salt. Mix thoroughly. Now apply the batter to each eggplant slice evenly. Dip the battered slices in the mix to coat it evenly on all sides. Place eggplant slices on a clean and dry flat plate and spray oil on them. Preheat the Air Fryer to 360F. Then put the eggplant slices on the wire mesh and cook for about 8 min. Top the air fried slices with about 1 tablespoon of marinara sauce and lightly spread fresh mozzarella cheese on it. Cook the eggplant for another 1-2 min or until the cheese melts. Serve warm.

Nutritional Information:

Calories: 217, Fat: 11G, Carbs: 19G, Protein: 12g

Air Fryer Radish Hash Browns

Preparation Time: 20 minutes | Yield: 4 Servings

Ingredients:

- 1 pound Radishes washed
- 1 medium Yellow/Brown Onion
- 1 teaspoon Garlic Powder
- 1 teaspoon Granulated Onion Powder
- 3/4 teaspoon Pink Himalayan Salt (or Sea Salt)
- 1/2 teaspoon Paprika
- 1/4 teaspoon Freshly Ground Black Pepper
- 1 Tablespoon Pure Virgin Coconut Oil

Directions:

Wash Radishes well and cut off roots. Trim steams, leaving 1/4-1/2 inch. Use a Food Processor or Mandolin and slice the Radishes and Onions. Add Coconut Oil and mix well. Grease Air Fryer Basket. Add Radishes and Onions to Air Fryer Basket. Cook at 360 degrees for 8 minutes, shaking a few times. Dump Radishes and Onions back into Mixing Bowl. Add Seasonings to Radishes and Onions and cook at 400 degrees for five minutes, shaking half way through.

Nutritional Information:

Calories: 83, Fat: 4g, Carbs: 4g, Protein: 6g

Air Fryer Chicken Quesadilla

Preparation Time: 15 minutes | Yield: 4 Servings

Ingredients:

- Zero Carb Soft Taco Shells
- Chicken Fajita Strips
- Shredded Mexican Cheese
- Salsa (optional)

- 1/2 cup sliced green peppers
- 1/2 cup sliced onions

- Sour Cream (optional)

Directions:

Preheat Air Fryer on 370 degrees for about 3 minutes. Spray pan lightly with vegetable oil. Place 1 soft taco shell in pan. Place shredded cheese on shell. (you can use as much or as little as you'd like.) Lay out fajita chicken strips so they are in a single layer. Put your onions and green peppers on top of your chicken. Add more shredded cheese. Place another soft taco shell on top and spray lightly with vegetable oil. (I put the rack that came with the air fryer on top of the shell to hold it in place. If you don't, the fan will suck it up. Trust me on this one!) Set timer for 4 minutes. Flip over carefully with large spatula. Spray lightly with vegetable oil and place rack on top of shell to hold it in place. Set timer for 4 minutes. If it's not crispy enough for you, leave in for a couple of extra minutes. Remove and cut into 4 slices or 6 slices. Serve with Salsa and sour cream if desired.

Nutritional Information:

Calories: 190, Fat: 16G, Carbs: 7g, Protein: 8g

Tomato Basil Scallops

Preparation Time: 15 minutes | Yield: 2 Servings

Ingredients:

- 3/4 cup heavy whipping cream
- 1 tablespoon tomato paste
- 1 tablespoon chopped fresh basil
- 1 teaspoon minced garlic
- 1/2 teaspoon salt

- 1/2 teaspoon pepper
- 1 12 oz package frozen spinach thawed and drained
- 8 jumbo sea scallops
- vegetable oil to spray
- additional salt and pepper to season scallops

Directions:

Spray a 7-inch heatproof pan, and place the spinach in an even layer at the bottom. Spray both sides of the scallops with vegetable oil, sprinkle a little more salt and pepper on them, and place scallops in the pan on top of the spinach. In a small bowl, mix together the cream, tomato paste, basil, garlic, salt and pepper and pour over the spinach and scallops. Set the airfryer to 350F for 10 minutes until the scallops are cooked through to an internal temperature of 135F and the sauce is hot and bubbling. Serve immediately.

Nutritional Information:

Calories: 359, Fat: 33g, Carbs: 6g, Protein: 9g

Air Fryer Keto Low Carb Fried Chicken

Preparation Time: 30 minutes | Yield: 6 Servings

Ingredients:

- 2 1/2 lbs Chicken drumsticks
- 1/4 cup Coconut flour
- 1/2 tsp Sea salt
- 1/4 tsp Black pepper
- 2 large Eggs
- 1 cup Pork rinds (2.25 oz)
- 1 tsp Smoked paprika
- 1/2 tsp Garlic powder
- 1/4 tsp Dried thyme

Directions:

Stir the coconut flour, sea salt and black pepper in a medium shallow bowl. Set aside. In a second medium bowl, whisk together the eggs. Set aside. In a third bowl, mix the crushed pork rinds, smoked paprika, garlic powder and thyme. Dredge the chicken pieces in the coconut flour mixture, dip in the eggs, shake off the excess, then press into the pork rind mixture. For best results, keep most of the third mixture in a separate bowl and add a little at a time to the bowl where you'll be coating the chicken. That way, it won't get clumpy too fast. Preheat the air fryer at 400 degrees F (204 degrees C) for 5 minutes. Lightly grease the metal basket and arrange the breaded chicken on it in a single layer, without touching. Place the basket into the air fryer. Cook the fried chicken in the air fryer for 20 minutes, until it reaches an internal temperature of 165 degrees F (74 degrees C).

Nutritional Information:

Calories: 274, Fat: 15G, Carbs: 3g, Protein: 28g

Appetizers and Sides

Beetroot Chips

Preparation Time: 20 minutes | Yield: 4 Servings

Ingredients:

- 2 Medium Sized Beetroot
- 1/2 Tsp Oil
- Salt to taste
- Pepper Optional

Directions:

Wash the Beetroot, peel the skin and set the skin aside. Using a mandoline slicer, slice them thin. Alternatively, if you don't have a slicer, slice them uniformly thin with your knife. Spread the beetroot slices on the paper and place another paper on top of it. Keep it aside for 10 minutes. This process will enable to absorb any extra moisture on the beetroot thins. Sprinkle the required amount of salt on the beetroot. Preheat the Airfryer to 150 C for 4 minutes. Pull the basket from the air fryer and place the chips in them. Slide it back in the air fryer and fry for 15 minutes. Make sure to remove in between after every 5 minutes and give it a good shake. Once the chips are slightly crisp on the outer edges and tender in the middle, allow them to cool down for some time. Slide the basket with the chips back again and heat at 180 C for another 3 minutes. The chips will be really crisp overall and perfect to munch right away. Season with Sea Salt and freshly ground pepper if you like or just munch it as it is. We love it either way.

Nutritional Information:

Calories: 150, Fat: 8g, Carbs: 20g, Protein: 4g

Air-Fried Shishito Peppers

Preparation Time: 10 minutes | Yield: 4 Servings

Ingredients:

- 16 oz bag Shishito peppers
- salt and pepper to taste
- 1/2 tbsp avocado oil
- 1/3 cup Asiagio Cheese grated fine
- Limes

Directions:

Rinse peppers with water and pat dry with paper towel. Place in bowl and toss with avocado oil, salt, and pepper. Place in air fryer and cook at 350 for 10 minutes. Watch carefully. You want them to come out blistered looking but not burnt. Place shishito peppers on serving platter. Drizzle with a little lime juice and top with grated asiago cheese. Serve!

Nutritional Information:

Calories: 63, Fat: 4g, Carbs: 1g, Protein: 3g

Air-Fryer French Fries

Preparation Time: 20 minutes | Yield: 2 Servings

Ingredients:

- 3 medium potatoes, whole, unpeeled
- 1/4 teaspoon garlic powder/ granulated garlic
- salt and pepper to taste
- 1 1/2 tablespoons oil of choice (Coconut also works well.)

Directions:

Wash your potatoes, and pat them dry. Slice your potatoes to the size fries you want, and try to be somewhat consistent with the size to allow for even cooking. (Note: larger fries may require slightly more cook time.) Toss your fries with the oil, garlic, salt and pepper. You can toss them in a bowl, or toss them in your air fryer basket. Cook them on 400 in the air fryer for about 20 minutes (more for larger, steak fries), and toss them around a couple times during the cooking to help evenly cook. Taste to see if you need more salt and pepper.

Nutritional Information:

Calories: 278, Fat: 10g, Carbs: 40g, Protein: 8g

Coconut Shrimp With Spicy Marmalade Sauce

Preparation Time: 20 minutes | Yield: 2 Servings

Ingredients:

- 8 large shrimp shelled and deveined
- 8 ounces coconut milk
- 1/2 cup shredded sweetened coconut
- 1/2 cup panko bread
- 1/2 teaspoon cayenner pepper
- 1/4 teaspoon kosher salt
- 1/4 teaspoon fresh ground pepper
- 1/2 cup orange marmalade
- 1 tablespoon honey
- 1 teaspoon mustard
- 1/4 teaspoon hot sauce

Directions:

Clean the shrimp and set aside. In a small bowl, whisk the coconut milk and season with salt and pepper. Set aside. In a separate small bowl, whisk together the coconut, panko, cayenne pepper, salt and pepper. One at a time, dip the shrimp in the coconut milk, the panko and then place in the basket of the fryer. Repeat until all the shrimp are coated. Cook the shrimp in the fryer for 20 minutes at 350 degrees or until the shrimp are cooked through. While the shrimp are cooking, whisk together the marmalade, honey, mustard and hot sauce. Serve the shrimp with the sauce immediately.

Nutritional Information:

Calories: 623, Fat: 21g, Carbs: 76g, Protein: 15g

Air Fryer Baked Sweet Potato

Preparation Time: 40 minutes | Yield: 3 Servings

Ingredients:

- 3 sweet potatoes
  1 tablespoon olive oil
- 1-2 teaspoons kosher salt

Directions:

Wash your sweet potatoes and then create air holes with a fork in the potatoes. Sprinkle them with the olive oil & salt, then rub evenly on the potatoes. Once the potatoes are coated place them into the basket for the Air Fryer and place into the machine. Cook your potatoes at 392 degrees for 35-40 minutes or until fork tender. Top with your favorites!

Nutritional Information:

Calories: 152, Fat: 4g, Carbs: 26g, Protein: 2g

Jalapeño Poppers

Preparation Time: 20 minutes | Yield: 4 Servings

Ingredients:

- 10 jalapeno peppers halved and deseeded
- 8 oz of cream cheese (you can use a dairy-free cream cheese)
- 1/4 c fresh parsley
- 3/4 c gluten-free tortilla or bread crumbs

Directions:

Mix together 1/2 of crumbs and cream cheese. Once combined add in the parsley. Stuff each pepper with this mixture. Gently press the tops of the peppers into the remaining 1/4 c of crumbs to create the top coating. Cook in an air fryer at 370 degrees F for 6-8 minutes OR in a conventional oven at 375 degrees F for 20 minutes. Let cool and ENJOY!

Nutritional Information:

Calories: 152, Fat: 10g, Carbs: 45g, Protein: 4g

Pork Taquitos

Preparation Time: 20 minutes | Yield: 2 Servings

Ingredients:

- 3 cups cooked shredded pork tenderloin or chicken
- 2 1/2 cups fat free shredded mozzarella
- 10 small flour tortillas
- 1 lime, juiced
- Cooking spray

Directions:

Preheat air fryer to 380 degrees. Sprinkle lime juice over pork and gently mix around. Microwave 5 tortillas at a time with a damp paper towel over it for 10 seconds, to soften. Add 3 oz. of pork and 1/4 cup of cheese to a tortilla. Tightly and gently roll up the tortillas. Line tortillas on a greased foil lined pan. Spray an even coat of cooking spray over tortillas. Air Fry for 7-10 minutes until tortillas are a golden color, flipping half way through. 2 taquitos per serving.

Nutritional Information:

Calories: 256, Fat: 4g, Carbs: 23g

Taco Bell Crunch Wraps

Preparation Time: 20 minutes | Yield: 4 Servings

Ingredients:

- 2 lbs ground beef
- 2 Tbps. Taco Seasoning
- 1 1/3 c water
- 6 flour tortillas, 12 inch
- 3 roma tomatoes
- 12 oz nacho cheese
- 2 c lettuce, shredded
- 2 c Mexican blend cheese
- 2 c sour cream
- 6 tostadas
- Olive oil or butter spray

Directions:

Preheat air fryer to 400. Prepare ground beef according to taco seasoning packet. In the center of each flour tortilla with 2/3 c of beef, 4 tbs of nacho cheese, 1 tostada, 1/3 c sour cream, 1/3 c of lettuce. 1/6th of the tomatoes and 1/3 c cheese. To close, flood the edges up, over the center, it should look sort of like a pinwheel. Repeat 2 and 3 with remaining wraps. Lay seam side down in your air fryer. Spray with oil. Cook for 2 mins or until brown. Using a spatula, carefully flip and spray again. Cook an additional 2 mins and repeat with remaining wraps. Allow to cool a few mins and enjoy.

Nutritional Information:

Calories: 954, Fat: 30g, Carbs: 34g, Protein: 42g

Panko Breaded Chicken Parmesan With Marinara Sauce

Preparation Time: 30 minutes | Yield: 4 Servings

Ingredients:

- 16 oz skinless chicken breasts sliced in half to make 4 breasts
- 1 cup panko bread crumbs
- 1/2 cup parmesan cheese grated
- 1/2 cup mozarella cheese shredded

- 3/4 cup marinara sauce
- 2 tsp Italian seasoning
- salt and pepper to taste
- cooking spray
- 1/8 cup egg whites

Directions:

Preheat the Air Fryer to 400. Spray the basket with cooking spray. Slice the chicken breasts in half horizontally to create 4 thinner chicken breasts. Place the chicken breasts on a hard surface and pound them to completely flatten. Grate the parmesan cheese. Combine the panko breadcrumbs, cheese, and seasonings in a bowl large enough to dip the chicken breasts. Stir to combine. Place the egg whites in a bowl large enough to dip the chicken. Dip the chicken in the egg whites and then the breadcrumbs mixture. Place in the Air Fryer. Spray the top of the chicken with cooking spray. Cook for 7 minutes. Top each of the breasts with marinara sauce and the shredded mozzarella. Cook for an additional 3 minutes or until cheese has melted.

Nutritional Information:

Calories: 332, Fat: 12g, Carbs: 13g, Protein: 37g

Apple Cinnamon Dessert Empanadas

Preparation Time: 30 minutes | Yield: 12 Servings

Ingredients:

- 12 empanada wrappers

- 1 tsp cinnamon

- 2 apples diced, I used one red and 1 green
- 2 tbsp raw honey
- 1 tsp vanilla extract
- 1/8 tsp nutmeg
- 1 tsp olive oil spray
- 2 tsp cornstarch
- 1 tsp water

Directions:

Place a saucepan on medium-high heat. Add the apples, cinnamon, nutmeg, honey, and vanilla. Stir and cook for 2-3 minutes until the apples are soft. Mix the cornstarch and water in a small bowl. Add to the pan and stir. Cook for 30 seconds. Lay the empanada wrappers on a flat surface. Add the apple mixture to each. Close the empanadas. Roll the empanada in half. Pinch the crust along each of the edges. Roll each of the sides inward. Continue to twist the crust until closed. Add the empanadas to the Air Fryer basket. It's ok to stack the empanadas. Place the Air Fryer on 400 degrees. Cook for 8 minutes. Turn and flip the empanadas. Cook for an additional 10 minutes. Cool before serving.

Nutritional Information:

Calories: 164, Fat: 5g, Carbs: 28g, Protein: 3g

Keto Appetizers and Sides

Air Fryer Zucchini Fries

Preparation Time: 15 minutes │ Yield: 4 Servings

Ingredients:

- 2 zucchinis large
- 1/4 cup coconut flour
- 1 tablespoon nutritonal yeast
- 1 teaspoon garlic powder
- 1 teaspoon onion powder
- 1/2 teaspoon salt
- 1/2 teaspoon Italian seasoning
- 1/4 teaspoon pepper

Directions:

Preheat air fryer to 400 degrees. Wash and dry zucchini. Cut the ends off and then cut each zucchini in half. Cut each half into 1/2 inch thick wedges. In a large mixing bowl, combine coconut flour, nutritional yeast, garlic powder, onion powder, salt, pepper and Italian seasoning. Mix thoroughly. Working in batches, toss zucchini wedges in coconut flour mixture until evenly coated. Arrange zucchini wedges in a single layer in fryer basket, skin side down. Do not overlap wedges. Depending on the size of your air fryer, you may need to work in batches. "Fry" in 400 degree air fryer for 15 minutes or until wedges are crispy and golden brown (no longer than 20 minutes). Serve with sugar-free ketchup, marinara or pizza sauce.

Nutritional Information:

Calories: 213, Fat: 12G, Carbs: 12G, Protein: 13g

Roasted Turnips

Preparation Time: 10 minutes │ Yield: 4 Servings

Ingredients:

- 4 medium turnips
- 2 teaspoons avocado oil
- 1 teaspoon sea salt
- 1 teaspoon cracked pepper
- 2 teaspoons minced parsley

- 1 1/2 teaspoon paprika

Directions:

Preheat the air fryer to 390 degrees or the oven to 450 degrees. Peel and dice the turnips and place them in a medium mixing bowl. Add the avocado oil, paprika, sea salt, and pepper to the bowl and toss to coat. Spread the turnips in an even layer in the air fryer basket or on a large baking sheet. Air fry for 10 minutes, shaking the basket once halfway through cooking. Sprinkle with parsley just before serving.

Nutritional Information:

Calories: 51, Fat: 3g, Carbs: 9g, Protein: 1G

Keto Air-Fried Pickles

Preparation Time: 15 minutes | Yield: 4 Servings

Ingredients:

- 1/2 cup crushed pork rinds
- 3 tablespoons Parmesan cheese
- 16 sliced dill pickles
- 1/2 cup almond flour
- 1 large egg beaten
- 1 teaspoon olive oil cooking spray

Directions:

Mix crushed pork rinds with Parmesan cheese in one bowl. In a second bowl add a whisked egg. In a third bowl add almond flour. Dredge each pickle in the almond flour, then in the egg, and finally in the pork rind mixture. Place in a greased air fryer to form one single layer of breaded pickles. Spray the tops with olive oil using an olive oil mister. Set air fryer timer to 6 minutes at 370 degrees Fahrenheit.

Nutritional Information:

Calories: 275, Fat: 19G, Carbs: 5g, Protein: 24g

Air-Fried Onion Rings

Preparation Time: 10 minutes │ Yield: 2 Servings

Ingredients:

- 1 Onion Sliced
- 1 1/4 cup Flour
- 1 tsp Baking Powder
- 1 Egg Beaten
- 1 cup + 1 tsp Milk
- 3/4 cup pork rind panko such as Pork King Good
- Seasonings of your choice

Directions:

Preheat your air fryer to 370 and lightly spray the basket for nonstick if needed. Set up a 'dredging' area by setting two shallow bowls side by side. A shallow dish or pan may works for the second area instead of using a bowl. In a mixing bowl, mix together the flour, baking powder and seasonings. Mix in the egg and then the milk (or beer). We will divide this by transferring half of this mixture to the first bowl in our dredging area. Now in the second bowl, or dredging area, place your pork rind panko. Using a fork, carefully take the first slice of onion and fully cover it with the contents of the first bowl- using a dredging technique. Then dip this piece into the pork rind panko. Place the covered slices of onion into the fryer basket, being careful to not overlap if possible. When the first bowl runs out of its contents, simply refill it with the leftovers from the mixing bowl. Tip- spray the onion rings with a bit of spray oil or something similar before placing the ring into the fryer. This will help them become crisp-like. Air fry the onion rings for 8 minutes and then flip them over. Continue to air fry for another 8 minutes or until done.

Nutritional Information:

Calories: 411, Fat: 2G, Carbs: 12G, Protein: 5g

Air Fryer Avocado Fries

Preparation Time: 10 minutes │ Yield: 2 Servings

Ingredients:

- 1 egg
- 1/2 cup pork rind panko such as Pork King Good
- 1 avocado
- 1/2 teaspoon salt

Directions:

Get a ripe but firm avocado. Cut in half and remove the pit. Cut avocado into wedges. Beat the egg with salt in one bowl. Add panko into another bowl. Dip wedges into the egg mixture, and then in to the pork rind panko. Place wedges into preheated to 400F air fryer in a single layer for 8-10 minutes. Shake half way through. They are done when lightly brown.

Nutritional Information:

Calories: 251, Fat: 17G, Carbs: 15G, Protein: 6g

Air-Fried Okra

Preparation Time: 15 minutes | Yield: 4 Servings

Ingredients:

- 7-8 ounces fresh okra
- 1 egg
- 1 cup skim milk
- 1 cup pork rind panko
- 1/2 teaspoon sea salt
- oil for misting or cooking spray

Directions:

Remove stem ends from okra and cut in 1/2 inch slices. In a medium bowl, beat together egg and milk. Add okra slices and stir to coat. In a sealable plastic bag or container with lid, mix together the pork rind panko and salt. Remove okra from egg mixture, letting excess drip off, and transfer into bag with pork rind panko. Be sure okra is well drained before placing it in the pork rind panko. You may want to use a slotted spoon to lift a little okra at a time and let plenty of the egg wash drip off before putting it into pork rind panko. Shake okra in crumbs to coat well. Place all of the coated okra into air fryer basket and mist with oil or cooking spray. Okra does not have to be in a single later, and it isn't necessary to spray all sides at this point. A good spritz on top will do. Cook at 390 F for 5 minutes. Shake basket to redistribute and give it another oil spritz as you shake. Cook 5 more minutes. Shake and spray again. Cook for 2 to 5 minutes longer or until golden brown and crispy.

Nutritional Information:

Calories: 241, Fat: 18G, Carbs: 15G, Protein: 4g

Baked Chicken Nuggets

Preparation Time: 25 minutes | Yield: 4 Servings

Ingredients:

- 1 Pound Free-range boneless, skinless chicken breast
- Pinch sea salt
- 1 tsp Sesame oil
- 1/4 Cup Coconut flour

- 1/2 tsp Ground ginger
- 4 Egg whites
- 6 Tbsp Toasted sesame seeds
- Cooking spray of choice

For the dip:

- 2 Tbsp Natural creamy almond butter
- 4 tsp Coconut aminos (or GF soy sauce)
- 1 Tbsp Water

- 1 tsp Sriracha, or to taste
- 1/2 tsp Ground ginger
- 1/2 tsp Monkfruit (omit for whole30)
- 2 tsp Rice vinegar

Directions:

Preheat you air fryer to 400 degrees for 10 minutes. While the air fryer heats, cut the chicken into nuggets (about 1 inch pieces,) dry them off and place them in a bowl. Toss with salt and sesame oil until coated. Place the coconut flour and ground ginger in a large Ziploc bag and shake to combine. Add the chicken and shake until coated. Place the egg whites in a large bowl and add in the chicken nuggets, tossing until they are all well coated in the egg. Place the sesame seeds in a large Ziploc bag. Shake any excess egg off the chicken and add the nuggets into the bag, shake until well coated. GENEROUSLY spray the mesh air fryer basket with cooking spray. Place the nuggets into the basket, making sure to not crowd them or they won't get crispy. Spray with a touch of cooking spray. Cook for 6 minutes. Flip each nugget and spray for cooking spray. Then, cook an additional 5-6 minutes until no longer pink inside, with a crispy outside. While the nuggets cook, whisk all the sauce ingredients together in a medium bowl until smooth. Serve the nuggets with the dip and devour!

Nutritional Information:

Calories: 250, Fat: 18G, Carbs: 6g, Protein: 25g

Air Fryer Egg Cups

Preparation Time: 30 minutes | Yield: 4 Servings

Ingredients:

- Non-stick cooking spray
- 4 large eggs
- 1 cup diced vegetables of choice
- 1 cup shredded cheese
- 4 Tbs half and half
- 1 Tbs chopped cilantro
- Salt and Pepper

Directions:

Grease 4 ramekins. In a medium bowl, whisk eggs, vegetables, half the cheese, half and half, cilantro, and salt and pepper together. Divide between the ramekins. Place ramekins in the air-fryer basket, set temperature to 300 degrees F for 12 minutes. Top the cups with remaining cheese. Set air-fryer to 400 degrees F, cook 2 minutes until cheese is melted and lightly browned. Serve immediately.

Nutritional Information:

Calories: 195, Fat: 12G, Carbs: 7g, Protein: 13g

Air Fryer Frittata

Preparation Time: 15 minutes | Yield: 4 Servings

Ingredients:

- 2 large Eggs
- 1 Cup shredded chicken
- 1 tbsp chopped Spring Onions
- 1 tbsp chopped Bell Peppers
- 2 tbsp Cheddar cheese
- 1 tbsp Melted Butter
- Salt and pepper to taste

Directions:

Generously grease a 4 inch cake pan or a mini loaf pan (or any oven safe pan that fits in your air-fryer basket) with butter. Add the chopped up breakfast sausage in the greased pan and air fry at 350F for 5 minutes. Meanwhile, in a medium sized bowl, crack 2 eggs. Add salt and pepper and whisk it well. Add the chopped spring onion, bell peppers and mix well. Once the sausage is cooked, add the egg mixture. Mix well with the sausages. Sprinkle with cheddar cheese and air fry at 350 F for another 5 minutes. Serve hot with fresh tomato salsa.

Nutritional Information:

Calories: 380, Fat: 27G, Carbs: 2G, Protein: 31g

Air Fried Blooming Onion

Preparation Time: 15 minutes | Yield: 4 Servings

Ingredients:

- 1 Onion
- 2.5 cups almond Flour
- 4 tsp Old Bay Seasoning

- 2 Eggs (Beaten)
- 1/2 Cup Milk

Directions:

Preheat your air fryer to 400 and prep your basket for nonstick if desired. In a bowl, whisk together your flour and seasonings. Now, in another bowl, whip together the eggs and milk (or liquid of choice). First pour the flour mixture over the onion and coat well. It is a good idea to get your hands involved and move the onion around in the bowl to help coat it. Or, you could cover the bowl with a plate or wrap and shake it to coat it. Lift the onion up and shake the excess flour mixture off back into the bowl. Move the onion over to the other bowl that contains the egg and milk and coat well. Use a spoon or ladle to help you coat the entire onion. Sprinkle the remaining flour mixture over the onion, shake the onion out again, and then place it into your air fryer. Air Fry this for 8-10 minutes or until crisp. Optional: For a bit of an oil taste, you can lightly spray your onion with a bit of olive or other oil before frying.

Nutritional Information:

Calories: 267, Fat: 20G, Carbs: 15G, Protein: 4g

Fish and Seafood Recipes

3 Ingredient Fried Catfish

Preparation Time: 60 minutes | Yield: 4 Servings

Ingredients:

- 4 catfish fillets
- 1/4 cup seasoned fish fry
- 1 tbsp olive oil
- 1 tbsp chopped parsley optional

Directions:

Preheat Air Fryer to 400 degrees. Rinse the catfish and pat dry. Pour the fish fry seasoning in a large Ziploc bag. Add the catfish to the bag, one at a time. Seal the bag and shake. Ensure the entire filet is coated with seasoning. Spray olive oil on the top of each filet. Place the filet in the Air Fryer basket. (Due to the size of my fillets, I cooked each one at a time). Close and cook for 10 minutes. Flip the fish. Cook for an additional 10 minutes. Flip the fish. Cook for an additional 2-3 minutes or until desired crispness. Top with parsley.

Nutritional Information:

Calories: 208, Fat: 6g, Carbs: 8g, Protein: 17g

Crumbed Fish

Preparation Time: 20 minutes | Yield: 4 Servings

Ingredients:

- 4 tablespoons vegetable oil
- 100g breadcrumbs
- 1 egg, whisked
- 4 fish fillets
- 1 lemon, to serve

Directions:

Preheat your air fryer to 180 degrees C. Mix the oil and the breadcrumbs together. Keep stirring until the mixture becomes loose and crumbly. Dip the fish fillets into the egg then shake of any residual. Dip the fish fillets into the crumb mix making sure it is evenly and fully covered. Gently lay in the air fryer then cook for 12 minutes. (Time may vary depending on the thickness of the fish). Serve immediately with lemon.

Nutritional Information:

Calories: 148, Fat: 7g, Carbs: 13g, Protein: 7g

Cajun Salmon

Preparation Time: 15 minutes | Yield: 2 Servings

Ingredients:

- 1 piece fresh salmon fillet (about 200g)
- Cajun seasoning (just enough to coat)
- A light sprinkle of sugar (optional)
- Juice from a quarter of lemon, to serve

Directions:

Preheat your airfryer to 180C. For the Philips airfryer, the orange light will go off to indicate that the temperature has been reached. For other brands, typically just preheat for 5 minutes. Clean your salmon and pat dry. In a plate, sprinkle Cajun seasoning all over and ensure all sides are coated. You don't need too much. If you prefer a tad of sweetness, add a light sprinkling of sugar. NO seasoning time required. For a salmon fillet about 3/4 of an inch thick, airfry for 7 minutes, skin side up on the grill pan. Serve immediately with a squeeze of lemon.

Nutritional Information:

Calories: 200, Fat: 12g, Carbs: 1g, Protein: 22g

Crunchy Air Fryer Sushi Roll

Preparation Time: 10 minutes | Yield: 3 Servings

Ingredients:

For the Kale Salad

- 1 1/2 cups chopped kale - ribs removed
- 1/2 teaspoon rice vinegar
- 3/4 teaspoon toasted sesame oil
- 1/8 teaspoon garlic powder

- 1/4 teaspoon ground ginger
- 3/4 teaspoon soy sauce
- 1 tablespoon sesame seeds - toasted or not - your call!

For the Kale Salad Sushi Rolls

- 1 batch Pressure Cooker Sushi Rice, cooked - cooled to room temperature

- 3 sheets of sushi nori
- 1/2 of a Haas avocado - sliced

Make the Sriracha Mayo

- 1/4 cup of your favorite vegan mayonnaise

- sriracha sauce - to taste

For the Coating

- 1/2 cup panko breadcrumbs

Directions:

Make the Kale Salad

In a large bowl, combine the kale, vinegar, sesame oil, garlic powder, ground ginger, and soy sauce. With clean hands, massage the kale until it turns bright green and wilted. Stir in the sesame seeds, and set aside.

Make the Kale Salad Sushi Rolls

Lay out a sheet of nori on a dry surface. With slightly damp fingertips, grab a handful of rice, and spread it onto the nori. The idea here is to get a thin layer of rice covering almost the entire sheet. Along one edge, you'll want to leave about 1/2" of naked seaweed. Think of this as the flap that will seal your roll shut. On the end of the seaweed opposite that naked part, lay out about 2-3 tablespoons of kale salad, and top with a couple of slices of avocado. Starting on the end with the filling, roll up your sushi, pressing gently to get a nice, tight roll. When you get to the end, use that naked bit of seaweed to seal the roll closed. If needed, get your fingertips wet, and moisten that bit of seaweed to make it stick. Repeat steps 2-3 to make 3 more sushi rolls.

Make the Sriracha Mayo

In a shallow bowl, whisk together the vegan mayo with sriracha, until you reach the heat level that you like. Start with 1 teaspoon, and add more, 1/2 teaspoon at a time, until you have the spicy mayo of your dreams!

Fry and Slice

Pour the panko breadcrumbs into a shallow bowl. Grab your first sushi roll, and coat it as evenly as possible in the Sriracha Mayo, then in the panko. Place the roll into your air fryer basket. Repeat with the rest of your sushi rolls. Air fry at 390F for 10 minutes, shaking gently after 5 minutes. When the rolls are cool enough to handle, grab a good knife, and very gently slice the roll into 6-8 pieces. When you're slicing, think of gently sawing, and don't press hard with your knife. That will just send kale and avocado flying out of the ends of your roll. Serve with soy sauce for dipping.

Nutritional Information:

Calories: 140, Fat: 2g, Carbs: 23g, Protein: 7g

BANG BANG Fried Shrimp

Preparation Time: 20 minutes │ Yield: 4 Servings

Ingredients:

- 1 pound raw shrimp peeled and deveined
- 1 egg white 3 tbsp
- 1/2 cup all purpose flour
- 3/4 cup panko bread crumbs
- 1 tsp paprika
- McCormick's Grill Mates Montreal Chicken Seasoning to taste

- salt and pepper to taste
- cooking spray
- Bang Bang Sauce
- 1/3 cup plain, non-fat Greek yogurt
- 2 tbsp Sriracha
- 1/4 cup sweet chili sauce

Directions

Preheat Air Fryer to 400 degrees. Season the shrimp with the seasonings. Place the flour, egg whites, and panko bread crumbs in three separate bowls. Create a cooking station. Dip the shrimp in the flour, then the egg whites, and the panko bread crumbs last. When dipping the shrimp in the egg whites, you do not need to submerge the shrimp. Do a light dab so that most of the flour stays on the shrimp. You want the egg white to adhere to the panko crumbs. Spray the shrimp with cooking spray. Do not spray directly on the shrimp. The panko will go flying. Keep a nice distance. Add the shrimp to the Air Fryer basket. Cook for 4 minutes. Open the basket and flip the shrimp to the other side. Cook for an additional 4 minutes or until crisp.

Bang Bang Sauce: Combine all of the ingredients in a small bowl. Mix thoroughly to combine.

Nutritional Information:

Calories: 242, Fat: 1g, Carbs: 32g, Protein: 37g

Airfried Salmon Patties

Preparation Time: 30 minutes | Yield: 4 Servings

Ingredients:

- 3 large russet potatoes (about 400g total)
- 1 salmon portion (about 200g)
- A handful of frozen vegetables (parboiled and drained)
- Chopped parsley
- 2 sprinkles of dill
- A few dashes of black pepper
- Salt to taste
- 1 egg
- Breadcrumbs to coat (you can use packaged panko or blend 4 pieces bread)
- Olive oil spray

Directions:

Peel and chop potatoes into small pieces. Bring a pot of water to boil and cook potatoes for about 10 minutes or til tender. Remove water and return potatoes to the pot on low flame. Let the water evaporate (about 2-3 minutes), taking care not to burn the potatoes. Mash with a whisk and transfer to a large mixing bowl. Refrigerate til no longer hot. In the meantime, prepare your breadcrumbs if not using packaged panko. Blend 4 pieces til fine but not overly so. Set aside. Airfry the salmon. Preheat AF for 5 minutes at 180C, then grill salmon for 5 minutes. Flake with a fork and set aside. Remove mash potatoes from fridge and add parboiled vegetables, flaked salmon, chopped parsley, black pepper, dill and salt. Do a taste test since everything is already cooked, and adjust seasonings to your liking. Add the egg and combine everything together. With dry hands, shape into 6-8 patties or smaller balls. Coat with breadcrumbs, spray some oil (make sure the breadcrumbs get oil on them if not the colour won't be nice), and AF at 180C til golden (about 10-12 minutes). If using the grill pan, there is no need to line with aluminium foil like I did. If lining with foil, you need to flip halfway once the top is golden. Serve with mayo and lemon with a salad on the side.

Nutritional Information:

Calories: 229, Fat: 8g, Carbs: 11g, Protein: 26g

Honey-Glazed Salmon

Preparation Time: 20 minutes | Yield: 4 Servings

Ingredients:

- 2 pcs Salmon Fillets (about 100gm each)
- 6 tbsp Honey
- 3 tsp Rice Wine Vinegar
- 1 tsp Water
- 6 tsp Soy Sauce

Directions:

Mix honey, soy sauce, rice wine and water together. Pour half (or some) of the mixture in a separate bowl, set aside as this will be used as sauce to serve with the salmon. Put together the salmon and the marinade mixture, let it marinate for at least 2 hours. Pre-heat the Airfryer at 180°C. Air-grilled the salmon for 8 minutes, flip over halfway and continue with additional 5 minutes. Baste the salmon with the marinade mixture every 3 minutes. To prepare the sauce, pour the remaining sauce in a pan and let it simmer for 1 minutes. Serve with salmon.

Nutritional Information:

Calories: 414, Fat: 23g, Carbs: 20g, Protein: 34g

Cajun Shrimp

Preparation Time: 10 minutes | Yield: 4 Servings

Ingredients:

- ½ pound tiger shrimp (16-20 count)
- ¼ teaspoon cayenne pepper
- ½ teaspoon old bay seasoning
- ¼ teaspoon smoked paprika
- 1 pinch of salt
- 1 tablespoon olive oil

Directions:

Preheat the air fryer to 390°F. In a mixing bowl, combine all of the ingredients, coating the shrimp with the oil and the spices. Place the shrimp into the cooking basket and cook for 5 minutes. Serve over rice.

Nutritional Information:

Calories: 457, Fat: 10g, Carbs: 51g, Protein: 37g

Spicy Fish Street Tacos with Sriracha Slaw

Preparation Time: 20 minutes | Yield: 2 Servings

Ingredients:

Sriracha Slaw:

- ½ cup mayonnaise
- 2 tablespoons rice vinegar
- 1 teaspoon sugar
- 2 tablespoons sriracha chili sauce

- ¼ cup shredded carrots
- 2 scallions, chopped
- salt and freshly ground black pepper
- 5 cups shredded green cabbage

Tacos:

- ½ cup flour
- 1 teaspoon chili powder
- ½ teaspoon ground cumin
- 1 teaspoon salt
- freshly ground black pepper
- ½ teaspoon baking powder
- 1 egg, beaten

- ¼ cup milk
- 1 cup breadcrumbs
- 12 ounces mahi-mahi or snapper fillets
- 1 tablespoon canola or vegetable oil
- 6 (6-inch) flour tortillas
- 1 lime, cut into wedges

Directions:

Start by making the sriracha slaw. Combine the mayonnaise, rice vinegar, sugar, and sriracha sauce in a large bowl. Mix well and add the green cabbage, carrots, and scallions. Toss until all the vegetables are coated with the dressing and season with salt and pepper. Refrigerate the slaw until you are ready to serve the tacos. Combine the flour, chili powder, cumin, salt, pepper and baking powder in a bowl. Add the egg and milk and mix until the batter is smooth. Place the breadcrumbs in shallow dish. Cut the fish fillets into 1-inch wide sticks, approximately 4-inches long. You should have about 12 fish sticks total. Dip the fish sticks into the batter, coating all sides. Let the excess batter drip off the fish and then roll them in the breadcrumbs, patting the crumbs onto all sides of the fish sticks. Set the coated fish on a plate or baking sheet until all the fish has been coated. Pre-heat the air fryer to 400°F. Spray the coated fish sticks with oil on all sides. Spray or brush the inside of the air fryer basket with oil and transfer the fish to the basket. Place as many sticks as you can in one layer, leaving a little room around each stick. Place any remaining sticks on top, perpendicular to the first layer. Air-fry the fish for 3 minutes. Turn the fish sticks over and air fry for an additional 2 minutes. While the fish is air-frying, warm the tortilla shells either in a 350°F oven wrapped in foil or in a skillet with a little oil over medium-high heat for a couple minutes. Fold the tortillas in half and keep them warm until the remaining tortillas and fish are ready. To assemble the tacos, place two pieces of the fish in each tortilla shell and top with the sriracha slaw. Squeeze the lime wedge over top and dig in.

Nutritional Information:

Calories: 192, Fat: 36g, Carbs: 20g, Protein: 17g

Zesty Ranch Air Fryer Fish Fillets

Preparation Time: 12 minutes | Yield: 4 Servings

Ingredients:

- 3/4 cup bread crumbs or Panko or crushed cornflakes
- 1 30g packet dry ranch-style dressing mix

- 2 eggs beaten
- 4 tilapia salmon or other fish fillets
- lemon wedges to garnish
- 2 1/2 tablespoons vegetable oil

Directions:

Preheat your air fryer to 180 degrees C. Mix the panko/breadcrumbs and the ranch dressing mix together. Add in the oil and keep stirring until the mixture becomes loose and crumbly. Dip the fish fillets into the egg, letting the excess drip off. Dip the fish fillets into the crumb mixture, making sure to coat them evenly and thoroughly. Place into your air fryer carefully. Cook for 12-13 minutes, depending on the thickness of the fillets. Remove and serve. Squeeze the lemon wedges over the fish if desired.

Nutritional Information:

Calories: 315, Fat: 14g, Carbs: 8g, Protein: 49g

Keto Fish and Seafood Recipes

Perfect Air Fried Salmon

Preparation Time: 25 minutes | Yield: 4 Servings

Ingredients:

- 2 wild caught salmon fillets with comparable thickness, mine were 1-1/12-inches thick
- 2 teaspoons avocado oil or olive oil

- 2 teaspoons paprika
- generously seasoned with salt and coarse black pepper
- lemon wedges

Directions:

Remove any bones from your salmon if necessary and let fish sit on the counter for an hour. Rub each fillet with olive oil and season with paprika, salt and pepper. Place fillets in the basket of the air fryer. Set air fryer at 390 degrees for 7 minutes for 1-1/2-inch fillets. When the timer goes off, open basket and check fillets with a fork to make sure they are done to your desired doneness. Notes: One of the beauties of the air fryer is that it's so easy to pop something back in for a minute if you want it cooked longer. You can also open it while it's cooking to make sure it's not overdone. I always set my timer for a little less so I can check on how things are coming along so I don't overcook an item. Things cook so fast sometimes a minute more is all it needs. Times for cooking will vary for salmon based on the temperature of the fish and the size of your fillets. Always set your air fryer for a little less time than you think until you become more used to the timing of your appliance.

Nutritional Information:

Calories: 237, Fat: 11G, Carbs: 1G, Protein: 34g

Air Fryer Salmon Cakes

Preparation Time: 7 minutes | Yield: 4 Servings

Ingredients:

- 8 oz fresh salmon fillet (could be from frozen)
- 1 egg
- 1/4 teaspoon garlic powder
- 1 sliced lemon
- 1/8 teaspoon salt

Directions:

Mince salmon in the bowl, add egg and spices. Form little cakes. Preheat air fryer to 390. Lay sliced lemons on the bottom of the air fryer basket. Place cakes on top. Cook for 7 minutes. Serve with your favorite dip, depending on your diet preferences.

Nutritional Information:

Calories: 288, Fat: 13G, Carbs: 13G, Protein: 26g

Air Fryer Coconut Shrimp

Preparation Time: 25 minutes | Yield: 4 Servings

Ingredients:

- 12 wild caught XL shrimp
- 1/3 cup almond flour
- 2 large eggs, beaten
- 1/2 cup unsweetened shredded coconut
- 1 lime wedge
- 1 tablespoon extra virgin olive oil

for brushing the basket.

Tropical Dipping Sauce

- 4 teaspoons coconut aminos
- 1 cup pineapple juice
- 1 teaspoon raw honey
- 1/4 teaspoon ginger powder
- 1/2 teaspoon tapioca starch

Directions:

Wash the shrimp and devein them. Make small slits in the belly of the shrimps, so they don't curl when cooked. Place almond flour on a plate, the eggs in a shallow bowl, and the shredded coconut on another plate. Dredge shrimp in the flour, dip in the egg and roll and coat with the shredded coconut. Refrigerate for 30 minutes. Preheat the air fryer to 360°F. Brush the basket with extra virgin olive oil. Place 6 shrimp in the basket, in a single layer, and set the timer for 7 minutes. Meanwhile, in a small saucepan, bring the pineapple juice to a boil and then simmer on low heat, until it's reduced to half. Add the rest of the ingredients and stir well. Take the pan off the heat and set aside. When the timer goes off, take the shrimp out, place them on a plate, and cover. Put the rest of the shrimp in the basket and cook for 7 minutes. When the timer goes off, squeeze some lime juice on the shrimp, and serve immediately with the Tropical Dipping Sauce.

Nutritional Information:

Calories: 250, Fat: 9g, Carbs: 13G, Protein: 20G

Air Fryer Crispy Fish

Preparation Time: 15 minutes | Yield: 4 Servings

Ingredients:

- 1 1/4 lb. cod
- 2 large eggs
- 1 cup almond flour
- 1 tbsp. dried parsley
- 1/2 tsp. garlic powder
- 1/2 tsp. onion powder
- 1/4 tsp. salt
- 1 tbsp. arrowroot powder (organic cornstarch works too)

Directions:

In a medium mixing bowl, beat the eggs with a whisk until well combined. In a separate, medium mixing bowl, mix together the almond flour, parsley, garlic powder, onion powder, salt and arrowroot powder (or cornstarch). Combine thoroughly. Dip the fish pieces into the egg and then roll in the coating, making sure to cover each part of the fish. Place the fish pieces in a single layer in the basket of the air fryer. Set to 350 for 7 minutes. When done, flip the pieces of fish in the basked and repeat for another 7 minutes.

Nutritional Information:

Calories: 338, Fat: 17G, Carbs: 12G, Protein: 35g

Air Fryer Parchment Fish

Preparation Time: 25 minutes | Yield: 2 Servings

Ingredients:

- 2 5-oz cod fillets thawed
- 1/2 cup julienned carrots
- 1/2 cup julienned fennel bulbs or 1/4 cup julienned celery
- 2 sprigs tarragon or 1/2 teaspoon dried tarragon
- 2 pats melted butter
- 1 tablespoon lemon juice
- 1 tablespoon salt divided
- 1/2 teaspoon pepper
- 1 tablespoon oil
- 1/2 cup thinly sliced red peppers

Directions:

In a medium bowl combine melted butter, tarragon, 1/2 teaspoon salt, and lemon juice. Mix well until you get a creamy sauce. Add the julienned vegetable and mix well. Set aside. Cut two squares of parchment large enough to hold the fish and vegetables. Spray the fish fillets with oil and apply salt and pepper to both sides of the fillets. Lay one filet down on each parchment square. Top each fillet with half the vegetables. Pour any remaining sauce over the vegetables. Fold over the parchment paper and crimp the sides to hold fish, vegetables and sauce securely inside the packet. Place the packets inside the air fryer basket. Set your air fryer to 350F for 15 minutes. Remove each packet to a plate and open just before serving.

Nutritional Information:

Calories: 251, Fat: 12G, Carbs: 7g, Protein: 3g

Lemon Garlic Shrimp

Preparation Time: 10 minutes | Yield: 4 Servings

Ingredients:

- 1 pound small shrimp, peeled with tails removed
- 1 Tablespoon olive oil
- 4 garlic cloves, minced
- 1 pinch crushed red pepper flakes (optional)
- 1/4 cup parsley, chopped
- 1/4 teaspoon sea salt

- 1 lemon, zested and juiced

Directions:

Heat your air fryer to 400°F. In a bowl, combine the shrimp, olive oil, garlic, salt, lemon zest, and red pepper flakes (if using). Toss to coat. Transfer the shrimp to the basket of your fryer. Cook for 5-8 minutes, shaking the basket halfway through, or until the shrimp are cooked through. Pour the shrimp into a serving bowl and toss with lemon juice and parsley. Season with additional salt to taste.

Nutritional Information:

Calories: 120, Fat: 5g, Carbs: 4g, Protein: 16g

Coconut Curry Salmon Cakes

Preparation Time: 25 minutes | Yield: 4 Servings

Ingredients:

- 1 lb Fresh Atlantic Salmon Side (half a side)
- 1/4 Cup Avocado, mashed
- 1/4 Cup Cilantro, diced + additional for garnish
- 1 1/2 tsp Yellow curry powder
- 1/2 tsp Stonemill Sea Salt Grinder

For the greens:

- 2 tsp SimplyNature Organic Coconut Oil, melted

- 1/4 Cup + 4 tsp Starch, divided (40g)
- 2 SimplyNature Organic Cage Free Brown Eggs
- 1/2 Cup SimplyNature Organic Coconut Flakes (30g)
- Organic Coconut Oil, melted (for brushing)

- Pinch of Stonemill Sea Salt Grinder
- 6 Cups SimplyNature Organic Arugula & Spinach Mix, tightly packed

Directions:

Remove the skin from the salmon, dice the flesh, and add it into a large bowl. Add in the avocado, cilantro, curry powder, sea salt and stir until well mixed. Then, stir in 4 tsp of the tapioca starch until well incorporated. Line a baking sheet with parchment paper. Form the salmon into 8, 1/4 cup-sized patties, just over 1/2 inch thick, and place them onto the pan. Freeze for 20 minutes so they are easier to work with. While the patties freeze, pre-heat your Air Fryer to 400 degrees for 10 minutes, rubbing the basket with coconut oil. Additionally, whisk the eggs and place them into a shallow plate. Place the remaining 1/4 cup of Tapioca starch and the coconut flakes in separate shallow plates as well. Once the patties have chilled, dip one into the tapioca starch, making sure it's fully covered. Then, dip it into the egg, covering it entirely, and gently brushing off any excess. Finally, press just the top and sides of the cake into the coconut flakes and place it, coconut flake-side up, into the air fryer. Repeat with all cakes. Gently brush the tops with a little bit of melted coconut oil (optional, but recommended) and cook until the outside is golden brown and crispy, and the inside is juicy and tender, about 15 minutes. Note: the patties will stick to the Air Fryer basked a little, so use a sharp-edged spatula to remove them. When the cakes have about 5 minutes left to cook, heat the coconut oil up in a large pan on medium heat. Add in the Arugula and Spinach Mix, and a pinch of salt, and cook, stirring constantly, until the greens JUST begin to wilt, only 30 seconds - 1 minute. Divide the greens between 4 plates, followed by the salmon cakes. Garnish with extra cilantro and devour!

Nutritional Information:

Calories: 211, Fat: 6g, Carbs: 2G, Protein: 34g

Air Fryer Parmesan Shrimp

Preparation Time: 15 minutes | Yield: 4 Servings

Ingredients:

- 2 pounds jumbo cooked shrimp, peeled and deveined
- 4 cloves garlic, minced
- 2/3 cup parmesan cheese, grated
- 1 teaspoon pepper
- 1/2 teaspoon oregano
- 1 teaspoon basil
- 1 teaspoon onion powder
- 2 tablespoons olive oil
- Lemon, quartered

Directions:

In a large bowl, combine garlic, parmesan cheese, pepper, oregano, basil, onion powder and olive oil. Gently toss shrimp in mixture until evenly-coated. Spray air fryer basket with non-stick spray and place shrimp in basket. Cook at 350 degrees for 8-10 minutes or until seasoning on shrimp is browned. Squeeze the lemon over the shrimp before serving.

Nutritional Information:

Calories: 102, Fat: 9g, Carbs: 4g, Protein: 5g

Keto Air Fryer Shrimp Scampi

Preparation Time: 15 minutes | Yield: 4 Servings

Ingredients:

- 4 tablespoons butter
- 1 tablespoon lemon juice
- 1 tablespoon minced garlic
- 2 teaspoons red pepper flakes
- 1 tablespoon chopped chives or 1 teaspoon dried chives
- 1 tablespoon minced basil leaves plus more for sprinkling or 1 teaspoon dried basil
- 2 tablespoons chicken stock (or white wine)
- 1 lb defrosted shrimp (21-25 count)

Directions:

Turn your air fryer to 330F. Place a 6 x 3 metal pan in it and allow the oven to start heating while you gather your ingredients. Place the butter, garlic, and red pepper flakes into the hot 6-inch pan. Allow it to cook for 2 minutes, stirring once, until the butter has melted. Do not skip this step. This is what infuses garlic into the butter, which is what makes it all taste so good. Open the air fryer, add all ingredients to the pan in the order listed, stirring gently. Allow shrimp to cook for 5 minutes, stirring once. At this point, the butter should be well-melted and liquid, bathing the shrimp in spiced goodness. Mix very well, remove the 6-inch pan using silicone mitts, and let it rest for 1 minute on the counter. You're doing this so that you let the shrimp cook in the residual heat, rather than letting it accidentally overcook and get rubbery. Stir at the end of the minute. The shrimp should be well- cooked at this point. Sprinkle with additional fresh basil leaves and enjoy.

Nutritional Information:

Calories: 221, Fat: 13G, Carbs: 1G, Protein: 23g

Tomato Mayonnaise Shrimp

Preparation Time: 10 minutes | Yield: 4 Servings

Ingredients:

- 1 pound large 21-25 count peeled, tail-on shrimp
- 3 tablespoons mayonnaise
- 1 tablespoon ketchup
- 1 tablespoon minced garlic
- 1 teaspoon sriracha
- 1/2 teaspoon smoked paprika
- 1/2 teaspoon saltFor Finishing
- 1/2 cup chopped green onions green and white parts

Directions:

In a medium bowl, mix together mayo, ketchup, garlic, sriracha, paprika, and salt. Add the shrimp and toss to coat with the sauce. Spray the airfryer basket. Place the shrimp into the greased basket. Set airfryer to 325F for 8 minutes or until shrimp are cooked, tossing half way through and spraying with oil again. Sprinkle chopped onions before serving.

Nutritional Information:

Calories: 196, Fat: 9g, Carbs: 2G, Protein: 23g

Poultry Recipes

Chicken Parmesan

Preparation Time: 12 minutes | Yield: 4 Servings

Ingredients:

- 2 (about 8 oz each) chicken breast, sliced in half to make 4 thinner cutlets
- 6 tbsp seasoned breadcrumbs
- 2 tbsp grated Parmesan cheese
- 1 tbsp butter, melted (or olive oil)
- 6 tbsp reduced fat mozzarella cheese
- 1/2 cup marinara
- cooking spray

Directions:

Preheat the air fryer 360F° for 9 minutes. Spray the basked lightly with spray. Combine breadcrumbs and parmesan cheese in a bowl. Melt the butter in another bowl. Lightly brush the butter onto the chicken, then dip into breadcrumb mixture. When the air fryer is ready, place 2 pieces in the basket and spray the top with oil. Cook 6 minutes, turn and top each with 1 tbsp sauce and 1 1/2 tbsp of shredded mozzarella cheese. Cook 3 more minutes or until cheese is melted. Set aside and keep warm, repeat with the remaining 2 pieces.

Nutritional Information:

Calories: 251, Fat: 10g, Carbs: 14g, Protein: 31g

Air Fryer Sriracha-Honey Chicken Wings

Preparation Time: 12 minutes | Yield: 4 Servings

Ingredients:

- 1 pound chicken wings, tips removed and wings cut into individual drummettes and flats.
- 1/4 cup honey
- 2 tablespoons sriracha sauce
- 1 1/2 tablespoons soy sauce
- 1 tablespoon butter
- juice of 1/2 lime
- cilantro, chives, or scallions for garnish

Directions:

Preheat the air fryer to 360 degrees F. Add the chicken wings to the air fryer basket, and cook for 30 minutes, turning the chicken about every 7 minutes with tongs to make sure the wings are evenly browned. While the wings are cooking, add the sauce ingredients to a small sauce pan and bring to a boil for about 3 minutes. When the wings are cooked, toss them in a bowl with the sauce until fully coated, sprinkle with the garnish, and serve immediately.

Nutritional Information:

Calories: 303, Fat: 14g, Carbs: 23g, Protein: 18g

Tandoori Chicken

Preparation Time: 30 minutes | Yield: 4 Servings

Ingredients:

- Chicken leg With Thigh - 4

For the first Marinade

- Ginger paste - 3 tsp
- Garlic paste - 3 tsp

- Salt to taste
- Lemon juice - 3 tbsp

For the second Marinade

- Tandoori masala powder - 2 tbsp
- Roasted cumin powder - 1 tsp
- Garam masala powder - 1 tsp
- Red chili powder - 2 tsp
- Turmeric powder - 1 tsp
- Hung curd - 4 tbsp
- Orange food color - a pinch optional

- Kasuri Methi - 2 tsp
- Black pepper powder - 1 tsp
- Coriander powder - 2 tsp
- Notes - You can add a bit of Mustard oil to the second marinade to get the Pungent taste in the chicken if you wish.

Directions:

Wash the chicken legs and make slits in them using a sharp knife. Add chicken in a bowl along with the ingredients for the first marinade. Mix well and keep aside for 15 minutes. Mix the ingredients for the second marinade and pour them over the chicken. Mix well. Cover the bowl and refrigerate for at least 10-12 hours. Line the basket of the air fryer with aluminium foil. Pre heat to 230 degrees C. Place the chicken on the basket and air fry for 18-20 minutes, until slightly charred and browned. Serve hot with Yogurt mint dip and Onion rings.

Nutritional Information:

Calories: 178, Fat: 6g, Carbs: 2g, Protein: 25g

Zinger Chicken Burger

Preparation Time: 12 minutes | Yield: 4 Servings

Ingredients:

- 6 Chicken Breasts
- 1 Small Egg beaten
- 50 g Plain Flour
- 10 ml KFC Spice Blend
- 100 ml Bread Crumbs

- 1 Tsp Worcester Sauce
- 1 Tsp Mustard Powder
- 1 Tsp Paprika
- Salt & Pepper

Directions:

Mince your chicken in the food processor. In the food processor add your Worcester sauce, mustard, paprika and salt and pepper. Make your chicken into burger shapes and put them to one side. In one bowl have your egg; in another add your flour. In a third have your KFC spice blend mix with your bread crumbs. Cover your Zinger burgers in the flour, the egg and then the bread crumbs. Place in the Airfryer at 180c for 15 minutes or until the chicken is cooked in the centre.

Nutritional Information:

Calories: 549, Fat: 11g, Carbs: 28g, Protein: 78g

Garlic Parmesan Chicken Wings

Preparation Time: 20 minutes | Yield: 12 Servings

Ingredients:

- 2 lbs wings + drumettes
- 3/4 cup grated parmesan cheese
- 2 tsps minced garlic
- 2 tsps fresh parsley, chopped
- 1 tsp salt
- 1 tsp pepper

Directions:

Preheat your air fryer to 400 degrees for 3-4 minutes. Pat chicken pieces dry with a paper towel. Mix parmesan cheese, garlic, parsley, salt and pepper together in a bowl. Toss chicken pieces in cheese mixture until coated. Place chicken in the bottom of the air fryer basket and set timer to 12 minutes. After 12 minutes, use tongs to flip chicken. Fry again for 12 minutes. Remove chicken from basket with tongs and sprinkle with more parmesan cheese and parsley. Serve with ranch, buffalo, or your favorite dipping sauce.

Nutritional Information:

Calories: 239, Fat: 20g, Carbs: 10g, Protein: 13g

Air Fryer Rotisserie Chicken

Preparation Time: 12 minutes | Yield: 4 Servings

Ingredients:

Brine:

- 1 Chicken OXO Cube
- 1 Tbsp Paprika
- 2 Tsp Thyme
- Salt & Pepper

Chicken Rub:

- 1 Tbsp Olive Oil
- 1 Tbsp Paprika
- 1 Tsp Celery Salt
- Salt & Pepper

Directions:

Place all of your brine ingredients into your freezer bag. Add the whole chicken and then fill with cold water until the chicken is fully covered. Zip it up and refridgerate it overnight. The next day when you are ready to cook your Air Fryer Rotisserie Chicken remove the chicken from the bag, remove the giblets, remove the brine stock and pat dry your whole chicken with some kitchen towel. Make your chicken rub in a small bowl. Place your whole chicken in the Air Fryer (breast side down) and rub ½ of the olive oil and ½ of the chicken rub into all visible skin. Cook the chicken for 20 minutes at 180c/360f. After 20 minutes turn over with kitchen tongs, then add the remainder of the oil and the chicken rub onto the other side of the chicken. Now cook for a further 20 minutes at the same temperature. Serve warm.

Nutritional Information:

Calories: 369, Fat: 17g, Carbs: 1g, Protein: 52g

Air-Fryer Garlic Parmesan Chicken Tenders

Preparation Time: 12 minutes | Yield: 4 Servings

Ingredients:

- 8 chicken tenders, raw
- 1 egg

- 2 tablespoons of water
- canola or non-fat cooking spray

For the dredge coating:

- 1 cup panko breadcrumbs
- 1/2 tsp salt
- 1/4 tsp ground black pepper, more or less to taste

- 1 tsp garlic powder
- 1/2 tsp onion powder
- 1/4 cup parmesan cheese

Directions:

Combine the dredge coating ingredients in a bowl big enough to fit the chicken pieces. In a second bowl large enough for dredging, place egg and water and whisk to combine. Dip chicken tenders into the egg wash and then into the panko dredge mixture. Place the breaded tenders into the fry basket. Repeat with remaining tenders. Place the Fry Basket into the Power Air Fryer XL. Spray a light coat of canola oil of non-fat cooking spray over the panko. Press the M button. Scroll to the French Fries Icon. Press the Power Button. Adjust cooking time to 12 minutes at 400 degrees.

Halfway through cooking, flip the tenders over. Notes: For best results, do not skip coating the chicken with your favorite cooking spray or turning them halfway through cooking.

Nutritional Information:

Calories: 220, Fat: 12g, Carbs: 6g, Protein: 27g

Air Fryer Pizza Stuffed Chicken

Preparation Time: 15 minutes | Yield: 2 Servings

Ingredients:

- 5 boneless skinless, chicken thighs
- 1/2 cup pizza sauce
- 14 slices turkey pepperoni
- 1/2 small red onion sliced
- 5 oz sliced mozzarella cheese
- 1/2 cup shredded cheese for topping

Directions:

Open your chicken thighs and lay them flat on a piece of parchment paper. Place a second piece of parchment paper over the chicken. Pound the chicken to create a thin piece. This makes the chicken easier to fold, and cook quickly. Spoon on a tablespoon of pizza sauce on each piece of chicken and spread it evenly. Place 3 pieces of turkey pepperoni on top of the sauce. Add one slice of Mozzarella cheese. Fold one side of the chicken over on to the other. Use a toothpick or skewer stick to hold the chicken together. Once cooked it stays together on its own. Preheat the air fryer at 370F for 2 minutes. Grease the tray, and lay the pieces out in a single layer. Add the chicken and let it cook for 6 minutes. Flip and cook for another 6 minutes. For the last 3 minutes, add cheese to melt on the top. Cooktime may vary depending on how thick your chicken pieces are. Always check chicken thighs to ensure they are heated to 165F.

Nutritional Information:

Calories: 195, Fat: 6g, Carbs: 3g, Protein: 31g

Air-Fryer Thai Peanut Chicken Egg Rolls

Preparation Time: 15 minutes | Yield: 4 Servings

Ingredients:

- 4 egg roll wrappers
- 2 c. rotisserie chicken shredded
- 1/4 c. Thai peanut sauce
- 1 medium carrot very thinly sliced or ribboned
- 3 green onions chopped
- 1/4 red bell pepper julienned
- non-stick cooking spray or sesame oil

Directions:

Preheat Airfryer to 390° or oven to 425°. In a small bowl, toss the chicken with the Thai peanut sauce. Lay the egg roll wrappers out on a clean dry surface. Over the bottom third of an egg roll wrapper, arrange 1/4 the carrot, bell pepper and onions. Spoon 1/2 cup of the chicken mixture over the vegetables. Moisten the outside edges of the wrapper with water. Fold the sides of the wrapper toward the center and roll tightly. Repeat with remaining wrappers. (Keep remaining wrappers covered with a damp paper towel until ready to use.) Spray the assembled egg rolls with non-stick cooking spray. Turn them over and spray the back sides as well. Place the egg rolls in the Airfryer and bake at 390° for 6-8 minutes or until they are crispy and golden brown. (If you are baking the egg rolls in an oven, place the seam side down on a baking sheet coated with cooking spray. Bake at 425° for 15-20 minutes.) Slice in half and serve with additional Thai peanut sauce for dipping.

Nutritional Information:

Calories: 235, Fat: 7g, Carbs: 17g, Protein: 21g

Air Fryer Chicken Nuggets

Preparation Time: 20 minutes | Yield: 4 Servings

Ingredients:

- 16 oz (2 large) skinless boneless chicken breasts, cut into even 1-inch bite sized pieces
- 1/2 teaspoon kosher salt and black pepper, to taste
- 2 teaspoons olive oil
- 6 tablespoons whole wheat Italian seasoned breadcrumbs
- 2 tablespoons panko
- 2 tablespoons grated parmesan cheese
- olive oil spray

Directions:

Preheat air fryer to 400°F for 8 minutes. Put the olive oil in one bowl and the breadcrumbs, panko and parmesan cheese in another. Season chicken with salt and pepper, then put in the bowl with the olive oil and mix well so the olive oil evenly coats all of the chicken. Put a few chunks of chicken at a time into the breadcrumb mixture to coat, then on the basket. Lightly spray the top with olive oil spray then air fry 8 minutes, turning halfway. Until golden.

Nutritional Information:

Calories: 188, Fat: 5g, Carbs: 8g, Protein: 25g

Air Fryer Lemon Pepper Chicken

Preparation Time: 15 minutes | Yield: 1 Serving

Ingredients:

- 1 Chicken Breast
- 2 Lemons rind and juice
- 1 Tbsp Chicken Seasoning
- 1 Tsp Garlic Puree
- Handful Black Peppercorns
- Salt & Pepper

Directions:

Preheat the air fryer to 180c. Set up your work station. Place a large sheet of silver foil on the work top and add to it all the seasonings and the lemon rind. Lay out your chicken breasts onto a chopping board and trim off any fatty bits or any little bones that are still there. Then season each side with salt and pepper. Rub the chicken seasoning into both sides so that it is slightly a different colour. Place it in the silver foil sheet and rub it well so that it is fully seasoned. Then seal it up very tight so that it cant breathe as this will help get the flavour into it. Then give it a slap with a rolling pin so that it will flatten it out and release more flavour. Place it in the air fryer for 15 minutes and check to see if it is fully cooked in the middle before serving. Serve.

Nutritional Information:

Calories: 140, Fat: 2g, Carbs: 24g, Protein: 13g

Nashville Hot Chicken

Preparation Time: 45 minutes | Yield: 8 Servings

Ingredients:

- 1/2 cup ranch dressing
- 1/4 cup finely chopped dill pickles
- 4 tablespoons butter, melted
- 1 tablespoon ground red pepper (cayenne)
- 1 tablespoon packed dark brown sugar
- 1 teaspoon salt
- 1 teaspoon black pepper
- 1 teaspoon chili powder
- 1 teaspoon garlic powder
- 1 teaspoon smoked paprika
- 2 lb fresh or frozen (thawed) chicken wingettes and drummettes

Directions:

In small bowl, mix ranch dressing and pickles. Cover and refrigerate sauce until ready to serve. In large bowl, mix melted butter, ground red pepper, brown sugar, salt, pepper, chili powder, garlic powder and smoked paprika. Place chicken in air fryer basket. Set to 350°F; cook 15 minutes, turning and stirring once. Transfer chicken to butter mixture in bowl; toss to coat. Return chicken to air fryer basket. Pour any remaining butter mixture over chicken. Set to 400°F; cook 12 to 15 minutes longer or until juice of chicken is clear when thickest part is cut to bone (at least 165°F), turning and stirring once. Serve with ranch dressing mixture.

Nutritional Information:

Calories: 320, Fat: 26g, Carbs: 4g, Protein: 19g

Air-Fried Buttermilk Chicken

Preparation Time: 15 minutes | Yield: 4 Servings

Ingredients:

- 800g store-bought chicken thighs (skin on, bone in)

Marinade

- 2 cups buttermilk
- 2 teaspoons salt
- 2 teaspoons black pepper
- 1 teaspoon cayenne pepper

Seasoned flour

- 2 cups all purpose flour
- 1 tablespoon baking powder
- 1 tablespoon garlic powder
- 1 tablespoon paprika powder
- 1 teaspoon salt

Directions:

Rinse chicken thighs to remove any obvious fat and residue, and pat dry with paper towels. Toss together chicken pieces, black pepper, paprika and salt in a large bowl to coat. Pour buttermilk over until chicken is coated. Refrigerated for at least 6 hours or overnight. Preheat airfryer at 180°C In separate bowl, combine flour, baking powder, paprika and salt and pepper. Remove the chicken 1 piece at a time from the buttermilk and dredge in seasoned flour. Shake off any excess flour and transfer to a plate. Arrange chicken one layer on the fryer basket, skin side up, and slide the basket into the airfryer. Set timer and air fry for 8 minutes. Pull out the tray, turn chicken pieces over, and set timer for another 10 minutes. Allow to drain on paper towels and serve.

Nutritional Information:

Calories: 320, Fat: 26g, Carbs: 13g, Protein: 19g

Copycat KFC Popcorn Chicken

Preparation Time: 15 minutes | Yield: 1 Servings

Ingredients:

- 1 Chicken Breast
- 2 ml KFC Spice Blend 60 ml Bread Crumbs
- 1 Small Egg beaten
- 50 g Plain Flour
- Salt & Pepper

Directions:

In the food processor blend your chicken until it resembles minced chicken. Set up a factory line with a bowl with your flour and a second bowl with your beaten egg. In a third bowl mix together your KFC spice blend, your salt and pepper and then your bread crumbs. Then like a factory line up make your minced chicken into balls and roll in the flour, the egg and then the spiced bread crumbs. Place in the airfryer at 180c for 10-12 minutes or until cooked in the middle.

Nutritional Information:

Calories: 44, Fat: 0g, Carbs: 3g, Protein: 2g

Chicken Tikkas

Preparation Time: 15 minutes │ Yield: 4 Servings

Ingredients:

For marinade-

- Boneless Chicken – 500 gms, cut into bite sized pieces.
- Thick yoghurt – 200 gms
- Bell peppers – 3 (any color of your choice), cut in an inch chunks.
- Cherry Tomatoes – 100 gms
- Fresh ginger garlic paste – 1 tbsp
- Red Chilli Powder – 2 tbsp

- Turmeric Powder – 1 tsp
- Coriander Powder – 2 tbsp
- Cumin Powder – 2 tbsp
- Olive oil – 2 tsp
- Salt to taste
- Garam masala powder – 1 tsp (adjust as per the spice you want)

For Garnishing –

- Fresh Coriander – ⅓ cup, chopped
- Fresh Mint Leaves – few

- Onion – 1, thinly sliced
- Lemon – 1, cut in half

Directions:

In a large bowl, mix together all the ingredients under marinade and coat the chicken well with spices. Cover and let it sit for 2 hours. If possible, overnight. Ask your children to help you in threading the chicken, tomatoes and peppers alternatively on the skewers and keep them ready. Preheat Air Fryer for 5 minutes at 200 Degrees C. Line the basket with aluminum foil and place the skewers. Grill for 12-15 minutes, turning each skewer once in between so it cooks evenly. Remove in a plate. Garnish with coriander, mint, onions and squeeze a lime before serving.

Nutritional Information:

Calories: 137, Fat: 3g, Carbs: 5g, Protein: 22g

Flourless Chicken Cordon Bleu

Preparation Time: 30 minutes | Yield: 2 Servings

Ingredients:

- 2 Chicken Breasts
- 1 Slice Cheddar Cheese
- 1 Tbsp Soft Cheese
- 1 Slice Ham
- 20g Oats
- 1 Small Egg beaten

- 1 Tsp Garlic Puree
- 1 Tsp Parsley
- 1 Tbsp Tarragon
- 1 Tbsp Thyme
- Salt & Pepper

Directions:

Preheat your air fryer to 180c. On a chopping board place your chicken breasts. Chop them at a side angle to right near to the corner so that you can fold them over and add ingredients to the centre. Sprinkle all sides of your chicken with salt, pepper and tarragon. In a mixing bowl add the soft cheese, garlic and parsley and mix well. Place a layer of the cheese mixture in the middle along with ½ a slice each of the cheddar cheese and the ham. Press down on the chicken so that it looks like it is sealed with a layer of filling inside it. In one bowl add the egg and in another add the blended oats. In the blended oats bowl also add the thyme and mix well. Roll the chicken in the oats first, then the egg and back in the oats. Place your chicken pieces on a baking sheet in your air fryer and cook for 30 minutes at 180c. After 20 minutes turn it over so that both sides have the chance to be crispy. Serve with new potatoes.

Nutritional Information:

Calories: 137, Fat: 3g, Carbs: 5g, Protein: 22g

Air Fryer KFC Chicken Strips

Preparation Time: 15 minutes | Yield: 8 Servings

Ingredients:

- 1 Chicken Breast chopped into strips
- 15 ml Desiccated Coconut
- 15 ml Plain Oats

- 75 ml Bread Crumbs
- 50 g Plain Flour
- 1 Small Egg beaten

- 5 ml KFC Spice Blend
- Salt & Pepper

Directions:

Chop up your chicken breast into strips. In one bowl add your coconut, oats, KFC spice blend, bread crumbs and salt and pepper. In another bowl have your egg and in another your plain flour. Put your strips in the plain flour, then in the egg and finally in the spicy layer. Place in the Air fryer at 180c and cook for 8 minutes and then cook for a further 4 minutes on 160c so that the chicken has plenty of time to cook in the centre. Serve.

Nutritional Information:

Calories: 94, Fat: 3g, Carbs: 13g, Protein: 4g

Pickle-Brined Fried Chicken

Preparation Time: 15 minutes | Yield: 4 Servings

Ingredients:

- 4 chicken legs (bone-in and skin-on), cut into drumsticks and thighs (about 3½ pounds)
- pickle juice from a 24-ounce jar of kosher dill pickles
- ½ cup flour
- salt and freshly ground black pepper
- 2 eggs
- 1 cup fine breadcrumbs
- 1 teaspoon salt
- 1 teaspoon freshly ground black pepper
- ½ teaspoon ground paprika
- ⅛ teaspoon cayenne pepper
- vegetable or canola oil in a spray bottle
- 2 tablespoons vegetable or canola oil

Directions:

Place the chicken in a shallow dish and pour the pickle juice over the top. Cover and transfer the chicken to the refrigerator to brine in the pickle juice for 3 to 8 hours. When you are ready to cook, remove the chicken from the refrigerator to let it come to room temperature while you set up a dredging station. Place the flour in the a shallow dish and season well with salt and freshly ground black pepper. Whisk the eggs and vegetable oil together in a second shallow dish. In a third shallow dish, combine the breadcrumbs, salt, pepper, paprika and cayenne pepper. Pre-heat the air fryer to 370°F. Remove the chicken from pickle brine and gently dry it with a clean kitchen towel. Dredge each piece of chicken in the flour, then dip it into the egg mixture, and finally press it into the breadcrumb mixture to coat all sides of the chicken. Place the breaded chicken on a plate or baking sheet and spray each piece all over with vegetable oil. Air-fry the chicken in two batches.

Place two chicken thighs and two drumsticks into the air fryer basket. Air-fry for 10 minutes. Then, gently turn the chicken pieces over and air fry for another 10 minutes. Remove the chicken pieces and let them rest on plate – do not cover. Repeat with the second batch of chicken, air frying for 20 minutes, turning the chicken over halfway through. Lower the temperature of the air fryer to 340°F. Place the first batch of chicken on top of the second batch already in the basket and air fry for an additional 7 minutes. Serve warm and enjoy.

Nutritional Information:

Calories: 542, Fat: 36g, Carbs: 6g, Protein: 46g

Air Fryer Southern-Style Chicken

Preparation Time: 15 minutes | Yield: 4 Servings

Ingredients:

- 2 cups crushed Ritz crackers (about 50)
- 1 tablespoon minced fresh parsley
- 1 teaspoon garlic salt
- 1 teaspoon paprika
- 1/2 teaspoon pepper
- 1/4 teaspoon ground cumin
- 1/4 teaspoon rubbed sage
- 1 large egg, beaten
- 1 broiler/fryer chicken (3 to 4 pounds), cut up

Directions:

Preheat air fryer to 375°. Spritz the air fryer basket with cooking spray. In a shallow bowl, mix the first seven ingredients. Place egg in a separate shallow bowl. Dip chicken in egg, then in cracker mixture, patting to help coating adhere. Place a few pieces of chicken in a single layer in the prepared basket, spritz with cooking spray. Cook 10 minutes. Turn chicken and spritz with additional cooking spray; cook until chicken is golden brown and juices run clear, 10-20 minutes longer. Repeat with remaining chicken.

Nutritional Information:

Calories: 405, Fat: 22g, Carbs: 13g, Protein: 36g

Air Fryer Ranch Chicken Tenders

Preparation Time: 15 minutes | Yield: 4 Servings

Ingredients:

- 8 chicken tenders, raw
- canola or non-fat cooking spray

For the Dredge Station:

- 1 cup panko breadcrumbs
- 1 egg
- 2 tablespoons of water

For the Ranch Chicken Seasoning:

- 1/2 tsp Salt
- 1/4 tsp Black pepper, more or less to taste
- 1/2 tsp Garlic powder
- 1/2 tsp Onion powder
- 1/4 tsp Paprika
- 1 tsp Dried parsley

Directions:

Preheat the Air Fryer. Warm the air fryer by setting it to 400 degrees F for 5 minutes. Allow it to run without any food in the basket. Set up a dredging station. Whisk the water and egg together in a shallow bowl. Pour the Panko Breadcrumbs in another shallow bowl. Prepare the Ranch Seasoning. In a small bowl, combine all the seasonings for the ranch seasoning. Season the Chicken. Sprinkle the chicken tenders with the ranch seasoning, turning to coat both sides. Dredge the chicken. Dip chicken tenders into the egg wash and then press it into the panko. Turn to coat both sides. Load the Fryer Basket. Place the breaded tenders into the fry basket. Repeat with remaining tenders. You may need to fry in batches. Fry the Chicken. Place the Fry Basket into the Power Air Fryer XL. Spray a light coat of canola oil of non-fat cooking spray over the panko. Press the M button. Scroll to the Fried Chicken Icon (400 degrees F). Press the Power Button. Adjust the cooking time to 12 minutes at 400 degrees. Halfway through cooking, flip the tenders over to brown the other side. The tenders are done when the center of the fattest part of the tender is 165 degrees F, the flesh is no longer pink, and the juices run clear.

Nutritional Information:

Calories: 197, Fat: 4g, Carbs: 12g, Protein: 25g

Keto Poultry Recipes

Air Fryer Chicken Breast

Preparation Time: 15 minutes | Yield: 4 Servings

Ingredients:

- 1 lb boneless skinless chicken breasts

Breading

- 1/4 cup pork rind panko
- 1/2 teaspoon salt
- 1/4 teaspoon black pepper
- 1/2 teaspoon paprika

- 1 tablespoon olive oil

- 1/8 teaspoon garlic powder
- 1/8 teaspoon onion powder
- 1/16 teaspoon cayenne pepper

Directions:

Heat air fryer to 390°F / 200 °C. Slice chicken breasts in half to make two thin chicken breast halves from each. Brush each side lightly with olive oil. Stir together the breading ingredients. Dredge the chicken breasts in the breading mulitple times until they are thoroughly coated. Shake off excess breading, and place in the air fryer (2 chicken breast halves at a time). Cook for 4 minutes, flip, then two more minutes. Cooking time will depend on the size and thickness of your chicken breasts, so cut one in half to see if they are done.

To prepare ahead. These air fryer chicken breasts may be cooked 2-3 days ahead and stored in the fridge. Place them back in the air fryer for 2-3 minutes until heated through and breading is crispy again.

Nutritional Information:

Calories: 188, Fat: 6g, Carbs: 5g, Protein: 25g

Air Fryer Baked Chicken Teriyaki Meatballs

Preparation Time: 25 minutes | Yield: 12 Servings

Ingredients:

FOR CHICKEN MEATBALLS

- 1 lb Ground/minced Chicken
- 1/2 cup Gluten-free Oats flour
- 1 small onion chopped (or 1/2 cup)
- 3/4 teaspoon Garlic powder or 3 fresh cloves
- 3/4 teaspoon Crushed chili flakes or chili powder (adjust according to taste)
- 1 teaspoon Dried cilantro leaves or use 1 tablespoon fresh
- Salt to taste

FOR SPICY TERIYAKI SAUCE

- 1/4 cup Sweet and sour sauce
- 2 tablespoon Rice Vinegar
- 2 tablespoon Soy sauce (light)
- 2 tablespoon Honey
- 1/2 teaspoon Hot sauce (optional)
- 1 teaspoon Crushed chili flakes
- 3/4 teaspoon Garlic powder
- 3/4 teaspoon Ginger powder

Directions:

Assemble ingredients for meatballs.

Ground chicken. Transfer everything to a bowl. Add oats flour. Knead until the mixture forms a dough. Form balls out of the dough. Arrange meatballs in air fryer basket. Bake at 350 degree F for 8-10 minutes. Remove from air fryer and let's prepare the sauce.

Assemble ingredients for the sauce.

Combine all the ingredients for teriyaki bowl in a pan. Whisk it well. On a medium-low heat, simmer sauce until it thickens. Add baked meatballs. Lightly mix until thoroughly coated with sauce. Garnish with sesame seeds, chopped scallions and serve hot.

Nutritional Information:

Calories: 47, Fat: 1G, Carbs: 4g, Protein: 3g

Air Fryer Honey Garlic Chicken Wings

Preparation Time: 35 minutes | Yield: 4 Servings

Ingredients:

- 2 lbs Chicken Wings About 16 drumettes and wingettes
- 1/2 cup Glucomannan Powder
- Kosher Salt
- 1 tbsp Unsalted Butter
- Garlic Powder Garlic-Honey Sauce

- 3 Garlic Cloves peeled and finely minced
- 1/4 cup stevia
- 1 1/2 teaspoons Soy Sauce
- Thinly Sliced Green Onions for garnish

Directions:

Pre-heat the air fryer to 375 degrees. Season the chicken wings lightly with kosher salt and dust with garlic powder on all sides. Place the Glucomannan Powder in a shallow bowl, then coat the chicken wings on all sides, shaking off any excess starch. Transfer the wings to the air fryer basket with room between them so they aren't touching to allow for the air to flow on all sides. Air fry the wings at 375 degrees for 20 minutes. Increase air fryer temperature to 425 degrees and continue to cook for 15 more minutes; turning the wings a few times while they cook to ensure even crisping.

To make the Sauce

While the wings are air frying, heat the butter and the garlic over medium-low heat in a small saucepan until it is melted, being careful not to brown the garlic. Stir in the stevia and soy sauce and continue to cook until the sauce thickens, about 10 minutes. Set the sauce aside and keep warm.

To Finish

When the chicken wings are crispy and cooked; transfer them to a warm bowl and mix with the desired amount of stevia-garlic sauce plus some thinly sliced green onions for garnish. Enjoy immediately.

Nutritional Information:

Calories: 175, Fat: 4g, Carbs: 10G, Protein: 24g

5-Ingredient Crispy Cheesy Air Fryer Chicken

Preparation Time: 15 minutes | Yield: 4 Servings

Ingredients:

- 4 thin chicken breasts (or two chicken breasts cut/pounded to be thin)
- 1 cup milk
- 1/2 cup pork rind panko breadcrumbs
- 3/4-1 cup shaved Parmesan-Asiago cheese blend (can use any type of hard shaved or shredded cheese like Parmesan, Asiago, Romano)
- salt + pepper to taste

Directions:

Preheat your air fryer to 400 degrees. Spray the cooking basket lightly with cooking spray. In a large bowl place the milk and chicken breasts. Sprinkle in a generous pinch of salt and freshly ground pepper. Allow to marinate in the milk for 10 minutes. In a shallow bowl combine pork rind panko breadcrumbs and shaved cheese. Dredge chicken breasts through panko and cheese mixture (press the mixture on top of the chicken generously) and place in the air fryer basket. Make sure that the basket is not overcrowded. I fit 2 chicken breasts in the basket, so I did this in two batches. Spray the top of the chicken lightly with cooking spray (this 'locks on' the cheesy bread crumb topping). Cook for 8 minutes, flipping the chicken breasts halfway through. Remove from the air fryer, repeat the process with any remaining chicken breasts. If you want to warm everything, you can add the already cooked chicken breasts into the basket and cook them for 1 minute to warm them! Enjoy

Nutritional Information:

Calories: 175, Fat: 4g, Carbs: 10G, Protein: 24g

Crispy Air Fryer Chicken Tenders

Preparation Time: 15 minutes | Yield: 4 Servings

Ingredients:

- 1 package (about 1 pound) chicken tenders
- 1/2 teaspoon all-purpose season salt
- 1/4 teaspoon freshly ground black pepper

- non-aerosol olive oil cooking spray
- 1/2 cup pork rind panko breadcrumbs

Directions:

Spray both sides of your chicken tenders with olive oil cooking spray. In a shallow bowl, whisk together the pork rind panko breadcrumbs, season with salt and pepper. Working in batches, press each tender into the crumbs and turn to coat. Shake off any excess and place onto a clean platter or cutting board and repeat. Spray the wire rack/basket (of your air fryer) to prevent sticking and preheat to 390°. Once preheated, work in batches of 3 or 4 tenders at a time, keep them from touching to avoid sticking. Cook for 3 minutes, use clean tongs to turn and repeat for 3 more minutes more. Transfer to a cooling rack before repeating with the remaining chicken tenders. To reheat, add all of the crispy (cooked) chicken tenders to the basket and heat at 390° for an additional minute or so.

Nutritional Information:

Calories: 188, Fat: 6g, Carbs: 5g, Protein: 24g

Keto Fried Chicken

Preparation Time: 50 minutes | Yield: 10 Servings

Ingredients:

- 5 pounds chicken about 10 pieces
- 1 cup almond milk
- 1 tablespoon white vinegar
- 2 cups crushed pork rinds
- 1/2 teaspoon salt
- 1/2 teaspoon thyme
- 1/2 teaspoon basil
- 1/3 teaspoon oregano
- 1 teaspoon celery salt

- 1 teaspoon black pepper
- 1 teaspoon dried mustard
- 4 teaspoons paprika
- 2 teaspoons garlic salt
- 1 teaspoon ground ginger
- 3 teaspoons white pepper
- 1 tablespoon coconut oil for air fryer only

Directions:

Place chicken in a large bowl. Mix almond milk and vinegar then pour over chicken. Let the chicken soak in the liquid for 2 hours in the refrigerator. In wide shallow bowl or dish, combine pork rinds, salt, thyme, basil, oregano, celery salt, black pepper, dried mustard, paprika, garlic salt, ground ginger, and white pepper. Dip each piece of chicken in dry pork rind mixture until coated.

Air Fryer:

Spread 1 tablespoon coconut oil in bottom of air fryer basket. Arrange chicken in single layer on basket. Air fry at 360°F for 10 minutes, rotate, then air fry another 10 minutes. Test chicken temperature to reach 165°F and continue cooking if needed.

Nutritional Information:

Calories: 539, Fat: 37g, Carbs: 1G, Protein: 45g

Air Fryer Whole Chicken

Preparation Time: 45 minutes | Yield: 6 Servings

Ingredients:

- 1 whole chicken
- 1 tbsp dry rub
- salt optional

- calorie controlled cooking spray or olive oil

Directions:

Preheat the air fryer to 180C / 350F. Pat chicken dry. Rub in the dry rub and sprinkle salt if desired. Spray air fryer with cooking spray. Add chicken in and cook for 30 mins on one side. Then flip and cook for 15-30 mins on other side depending on the size of your bird. It is important to check that the internal temperature of the chicken is 75C (165F) before serving.

Nutritional Information:

Calories: 412, Fat: 28G, Carbs: 5g, Protein: 35g

Air Fryer Chicken Wings With Buffalo Sauce

Preparation Time: 35 minutes | Yield: 5 Servings

Ingredients:

Wings:

- 2 pounds chicken wingettes
- 1 tablespoon olive oil or avocado oil
- 1/2 teaspoon garlic powder
- 1/2 teaspoon salt
- extra oil for greasing

Buffalo Sauce:

- 1/3 cup hot pepper sauce I used Frank's Red Hot
- 1/4 cup butter ghee for paleo
- 1 tablespoon white vinegar
- 1/8 teaspoon ground chipolte pepper or cayenne pepper

Directions:

Wings:

In a large bowl, rub olive oil on chicken wings and then sprinkle on the garlic powder and salt. Rub inside of air fryer basket with a little more olive oil, avocado oil, or coconut oil. Place chicken wings in a single layer in basket. Cook wings at 360°F for 25 minutes. Flip wings over. Then increase temperature to 400°F and cook for 4 more minutes.

Sauce:

While wings are cooking in air fryer, combine hot sauce, butter, vinegar, and ground pepper in small pot. Bring sauce to a boil on medium heat while whisking everything together. Remove from heat and set aside. When wings are done, add them to the sauce and coat each piece evenly. Serve with blue cheese dressing and celery.

Nutritional Information:

Calories: 327, Fat: 28G, Carbs: 0g, Protein: 18g

Keto Thai Chili Chicken Wings

Preparation Time: 25 minutes | Yield: 2 Servings

Ingredients:

- 16 chicken wings drummettes (party
- 1/2 cup almond flour
- McCormicks Grill Mates Chicken

wings)
- cooking spray I prefer to use olive oil or coconut oil
- 1/4 cup low-fat buttermilk

Seasoning to taste

Thai Chili Marinade

- 3 tbsp low-sodium soy sauce
- 1 tsp ginger I used ginger in a jar
- 3 garlic cloves
- 2 green onions
- 1 tsp rice wine vinger
- 1 tbsp Sriracha This amount produces a mild/medium spice. For spicier wings use more Sriracha.
- 1 tsp granulated erythritol sweetener
- 1 tbsp sesame oil

Directions:

Thai Chili Marinade: Combine all of the ingredients in a blender. Blend for 45- 60 seconds or until the mixture is of liquid consistency.

Chicken

Wash and pat dry the chicken. Place the chicken in a Ziploc bag and drizzle the buttermilk over the chicken. Season the chicken with the chicken seasoning. Place the Ziploc bag in the fridge to marinate for at least 30 minutes. I prefer overnight. Once the chicken has marinated, add the flour to a separate Ziploc bag. Add the chicken to bag with the flour. Shake to thoroughly coat the chicken. Spray the Air Fryer pan with cooking oil. I love to use olive oil or coconut. Using tongs, remove the chicken from the bag and place on the air fryer pan. It's ok to stack the chicken on top of each other. Spray cooking oil over the top of the chicken. Set the timer on the air fryer for 5 minutes at a temperature of 400 degrees. Allow the chicken to cook for 5 minutes. Remove the pan and shake the chicken to ensure all of the pieces are fully cooked. You can also turn each piece of chicken onto the other side using tongs. Allow the chicken to cook an additional 5 minutes. Remove the chicken from the pan. Glaze each piece of chicken with the Thai Chili marinade using a cooking brush. Return the chicken to the Air Fryer. Cook for 7-10 minutes. I allowed my chicken to cook for 10 minutes. Use your judgment here. Each Air Fryer brand is different. You can check in on your chicken at the 5-minute mark to ensure it has fully cooked on the inside. Cool before serving.

Nutritional Information:

Calories: 202, Fat: 11G, Carbs: 10G, Protein: 12g

Keto Adobo Air Fried Chicken Thighs

Preparation Time: 20 minutes | Yield: 4 Servings

Ingredients:

- 4 large chicken thighs
- 2 tbsp adobo seasoning
- 1 tbsp olive oil

Directions:

Add olive oil to bag or plate and coat chicken in it. Toss chicken thighs in adobo seasoning to coat. Place chicken thighs in air fryer basket, making sure they don't touch or crowd each other. Set air fryer to 350 degrees and set the timer to 10 minutes. After 10 minutes, flip chicken to other side and cook another 10 minutes. Chicken will be golden brown and 165 degrees internal temperature at the end of cooking.

Nutritional Information:

Calories: 359, Fat: 24G, Carbs: 1G, Protein: 36g

Jalapeno Popper Stuffed Chicken Breast

Preparation Time: 30 minutes | Yield: 4 Servings

Ingredients:

- 4 chicken breasts 4oz
- 2 jalapeños
- 4 oz cream cheese
- 4 oz cheddar cheese
- 8 strips bacon

Directions:

Butterfly chicken with a sharp knife, but don't cut all the way through. Spread cream cheese evenly on the inside of the chicken breasts. Divide jalapeño between the two chicken breasts. Top with the cheddar cheese. And close the chicken back up. Wrap each chicken breast with 2 slices of bacon. Place chicken in the air fryer, and turn air fryer on to 370 degrees for 20 minutes.

Nutritional Information:

Calories: 354, Fat: 42G, Carbs: 2G, Protein: 62g

Herb-Marinated Chicken Thighs

Preparation Time: 35 minutes | Yield: 4 Servings

Ingredients:

- 6-10 bone-in, skin-on chicken thighs
- 1/4 cup olive oil
- 2 T lemon juice
- 2 tsp. garlic powder
- 1 tsp. Spike Seasoning, or use any all-purpose herb blend.
- 1 tsp. dried basil
- 1/2 tsp. dried oregano
- 1/2 tsp. onion powder
- 1/2 tsp. dried sage
- 1/4 tsp. black pepper

Directions:

Trim some of the skin and most of the fat from the chicken thighs. (I used kitchen shears to trim the chicken.) I like to make short slits through the skin and into the meat, but that's not essential. Mix together olive oil, lemon juice, garlic powder, Spike Seasoning (or another seasoning blend), dried basil, dried oregano, onion powder, dried sage, and black pepper to make the marinade. Put chicken thighs in a Ziploc bag or plastic container with a snap-tight lid, add the marinade and let the chicken marinate in the fridge at least 6 hours, or all day while you're at work. When it's time to cook, drain the chicken well in a colander placed in the sink and discard marinade. Arrange chicken top-side down in the air fryer basket or on a baking rack and let the chicken come to room temperature while you preheat the air fryer to 360F/185C (if needed) or preheat the oven to 400F/200C.

TO COOK IN AIR FRYER: Cook chicken top-side down in the pre-heated air fryer for 8 minutes. Then turn the chicken thighs over and cook about 6 minutes more. After six minutes, check the chicken to see if some pieces are getting too browned and rearrange the chicken thighs in the air-fryer basket if needed. (I switched some of the outside more-browned pieces to the inside and I think some pieces would have burned if I hadn't done that.) Cook about 6 minutes more, or until the chicken is well-browned with crispy skin and the internal temperature is at least 165F/75C.

Serve hot. If you want to use the air fryer and need to cook two batches for a larger family, keep the first batch warm in a 200F/100C oven while the second batch cooks.

Nutritional Information:

Calories: 262, Fat: 10G, Carbs: 11G, Protein: 32g

Air Fryer Chicken Nuggets

Preparation Time: 20 minutes | Yield: 4 Servings

Ingredients:

- 1 pound Chicken Breast, cut into bite sized nugget shapes
- ¾ cup Almond Flour
- ¼ cup Ground Flax Seed
- 2 Eggs
- 1 tsp Salt
- ⅛ tsp Ground Black Pepper
- 1 pinch Paprika
- 2 tsp Avocado Oil
- 1 tsp Garlic Powder

Directions:

Grease the bottom of your air fryer with avocado oil and preheat your air fryer to 400. Grab 2 medium sized bowls: In one whisk the 2 eggs together. In another add flours and spices and whisk until fully combined. Add 2-3 nuggets to bowl with beaten eggs and fully coat before dredging in the breading mix making sure all sides of chicken are coated. Set aside on a plate until all of them are coated. Once all chicken nuggets are coated in egg and breading, place in your air fryer basket leaving room in between each piece of chicken so that air has a chance to flow through and make them crispy. Cook on one side for 10 minutes. Using tongs, carefully flip the chicken nuggets to cook for 10 more minutes or until fully cooked through.

Nutritional Information:

Calories: 232, Fat: 10G, Carbs: 3g, Protein: 25g

Bacon Wrapped Chicken Bites

Preparation Time: 10 minutes | Yield: 4 Servings

Ingredients:

- 1.25 lbs (3) boneless skinless chicken breast, cut in 1-inch chunks (about 30 pieces)
- optional, duck sauce or Thai sweet chili sauce for dipping
- 10 slices center cut bacon, cut into thirds

Directions:

Preheat the air fryer. Wrap a piece of bacon around each piece of chicken and secure with a toothpick. Air fry, in batches in an even layer 400F for 8 minutes, turning halfway until the chicken is cooked and the bacon is browned. Blot on a paper towel and serve right away.

Nutritional Information:

Calories: 98, Fat: 4g, Carbs: 0g, Protein: 16g

Air Fryer Chicken Parmesan

Preparation Time: 25 minutes | Yield: 4 Servings

Ingredients:

- 1 lb chicken breasts, pounded thin, sliced in half or 4 chicken cutlets at approx 4 oz each
- 3/4 cup blanched almond flour
- 2 tablespoons coconut flour
- 1 tablespoon Italian seasoning spice blend
- 1 teaspoon salt
- 1 teaspoon pepper
- 1 egg, whisked
- 4 slices fresh mozzarella cheese - omit if paleo/whole30
- 1/2 cup marinara sauce, plus more to taste
- cooking spray

Directions:

In a mixing bowl, combine almond flour, coconut flour, Italian spices, salt and pepper. Whisk well to combine. Add 1 whisked egg to another bowl. Dip chicken cutlet into egg wash, then dip into the almond flour breading. Make sure both sides are evenly coated with breading. Spray each breast with cooking spray, and add to basket of Air Fryer. Cook 8-10 minutes at 350F. Using tongs, flip sides, and top with marinara and mozzarella, if using. Cook 4-6 more minutes, until chicken is cooked through (will read at 165F). Repeat if making in batches (depending on basket size).

Nutritional Information:

Calories: 360, Fat: 20G, Carbs: 8g, Protein: 30g

Air Fryer Keto Chicken Meatballs

Preparation Time: 12 minutes | Yield: 20 Servings

Ingredients:

- 1 pound ground chicken
- 1 large egg, beaten
- ½ cup Parmesan cheese, grated
- ½ cup pork rinds, ground
- 1 teaspoon garlic powder

- 1 teaspoon paprika
- 1 teaspoon kosher salt
- ½ teaspoon pepper Breading
- ½ cup pork rinds, ground

Directions:

Preheat Air Fryer to 400° In a large bowl, combine chicken, egg, cheese, pork rinds (1/2 cup), garlic, paprika, salt and pepper. Roll into 1½- inch balls. Roll the meatballs in the ground pork rinds. Coat the air fryer basket with cooking spray, add meatballs in a single layer and cook for 12 minutes, turning once.

Nutritional Information:

Calories: 360, Fat: 20G, Carbs: 8g, Protein: 30g

Keto Southern Fried Chicken Tenders

Preparation Time: 25 minutes | Yield: 4 Servings

Ingredients:

- 4 Chicken Breasts

- 1/2 Tbsp Garlic Powder

- 5oz (150G) Almond Flour
- 1 Large Egg
- 1/2 Tbsp Cayenne Pepper
- 1/2 Tbsp Onion Salt
- 1/2 Tbsp Dried Mixed Herbs
- 1 tsp Salt
- 1 tsp Black Pepper

Directions:

Slice up your chicken into strips, about 5-6 pieces per breast. Lay your chicken strips out on a plate. Mix together all your dry ingredients, except for the almond flour. Make sure they are mixed well. Using half of the spice mix you want to coat the chicken evenly. You can do this by sprinkling it from a height of about two feet above the plate. Turn over the chicken and coat the other side. Hold back half of your spice mix for the next step. Combine your remaining spices with your almond flour in a bowl. In a separate bowl, whisk your egg well. Now it's time to make your tenders! Take the chicken one piece at a time, and dunk it into the egg, and then dunk it straight into the almond flour mixture. You will want to roll it around in the flour to make sure it is evenly coated. I'd recommend using tongs or another utensil for this, as the mixture can get pretty sticky and messy on your fingers. Place the coated chicken on a greased baking rack as you go. When you have all your chicken coated, you will pop the baking tray into the oven at about 350 degrees F (180C) for 22 mins, turning halfway through (Be careful that the coating doesn't stick to the rack and come away from the keto fried chicken).

Nutritional Information:

Calories: 365, Fat: 20G, Carbs: 4g, Protein: 38g

Chicken Strips Recipe

Preparation Time: 25 minutes | Yield: 4 Servings

Ingredients:

- 2 lbs boneless, skinless chicken tenderloins
- 1 cup almond flour
- 3 tbsp tapioca starch
- 1 1/2 tsp garlic salt
- 1 tsp salt
- 2 tsp Italian seasoning
- 1/2 tsp paprika
- 2 large eggs

Directions:

Mix together almond flour, tapioca starch, garlic salt, salt, Italian seasoning, and paprika in a shallow bowl. In a separate bowl, whisk together the eggs. Dip each chicken tenderloin in the eggs then dip in the almond flour mixture to coat. Repeat with all the tenderloins. Place the prepared chicken strips in a single layer in the basket of yourAir Fryer. Cook for 20 minutes at 360 degrees F. Check for doneness (ensure no pink in center). Serve with your favorite dipping sauce or pair with sweet potato fries.

Nutritional Information:

Calories: 112, Fat: 6g, Carbs: 7g, Protein: 7g

Chick-Fil-A Copycat Recipe

Preparation Time: 25 minutes | Yield: 8 Servings

Ingredients:

Keto Fried Chicken Tenders

- 8 Chicken Tenders
- 24oz Jar of Dill Pickles (you only need the juice)
- 3/4 Cup Now Foods Almond Flour
- 1 tsp Salt
- 1 tsp Pepper

- 2 Eggs, beaten
- 1 1/2 Cups pork panko (Bread Crumb Substitute)
- Nutiva Organic Coconut Oil for frying

Low Carb Copycat Chick-Fil-A Sauce

- 1/2 Cup Mayo
- 2 tsp Yellow Mustard
- 1 tsp Lemon Juice

- 2 tbs Honey Trees Sugar-Free Honey
- 1 tbs Organicville BBQ sauce

Directions:

Put chicken tenders and pickle juice in a large zip lock bag and marinate for at least 1 hour, preferably overnight. In a small bowl, mix almond flour, salt, and pepper. Create an assembly line of three bowls, one with almond flour mixture, the second with the eggs and the third with the pork panko. Dredge the chicken in the almond flour mixture, then in the egg and finally in the pork panko until well coated. Set the air fryer to 375 F and cook the chicken for about 15 minutes.

Low Carb Copycat Chick-Fil-A Sauce: In a small bowl, combine all ingredients and stir until fully combined.

Nutritional Information:

Calories: 193, Fat: 9g, Carbs: 5g, Protein: 26g

Crumbed Chicken Tenderloins

Preparation Time: 25 minutes | Yield: 4 Servings

Ingredients:

- 1 egg
- 1/2 cup pork rind panko breadcrumbs
- 2 tablespoons vegetable oil
- 8 chicken tenderloins

Directions:

Preheat an air fryer to 350 degrees F (175 degrees C). Whisk egg in a small bowl. Mix pork rind panko breadcrumbs and oil together in a second bowl until mixture becomes loose and crumbly. Dip each chicken tenderloin into the bowl of egg; shake off any residual egg. Dip chicken into the crumb mixture, making sure it is evenly and fully covered. Lay chicken tenderloins into the basket of the air fryer. Cook until no longer pink in the center, about 12 minutes. An instant- read thermometer inserted into the center should read at least 165 degrees F (74 degrees C).

Nutritional Information:

Calories: 253, Fat: 11G, Carbs: 9g, Protein: 26g

Meat Recipes

Stromboli

Preparation Time: 15 minutes | Yield: 4 Servings

Ingredients:

- 12 ounce pizza crust, refrigerated
- 3 cup cheddar cheese, shredded
- 0.75 cup Mozzarella cheese, shredded
- 1/2 pound cooked ham, sliced
- 3 ounce red bell peppers, roasted
- 1 egg yolk
- 1 tablespoon milk

Directions:

Roll the dough out until 1/4 inch thick. Layer the ham, cheese and peppers on one side of the dough. Fold over to seal. Mix the egg and milk together and brush the dough. Place the stromboli into the Fry Basket and place it into the Power Air Fryer XL. Press the M Button. Scroll to the Chicken icon. Press the Power Button & adjust cooking time to 15 minutes at 360 degrees. Every 5 minutes, carefully turn stromboli over.

Nutritional Information:

Calories: 329, Fat: 12g, Carbs: 34g, Protein: 18g

Roasted Stuffed Peppers

Preparation Time: 15 minutes | Yield: 4 Servings

Ingredients:

- 2 medium green peppers, stems and seeds removed - cooked in boiling salted water for 3 minutes
- ½ cup tomato sauce
- 1 teaspoon Worcestershire sauce
- ½ teaspoon salt

- ½ medium onion, chopped
- 1 clove garlic, minced
- 1 teaspoon olive oil
- 8 ounces lean ground beef
- ½ teaspoon black pepper
- 4 ounces cheddar cheese, shredded

Directions:

Preheat air fryer to 390 setting. Sauté the onion and garlic in the olive oil in a small nonstick skillet until golden and remove from burner to cool. Blend the beef, cooked vegetables, ¼ cup tomato sauce, Worcestershire, salt and pepper and half the shredded cheese in a medium bowl. Divide and stuff the pepper halves - top with remaining tomato sauce and cheese. Arrange in the air fryer basket and air fry or bake until meat is cooked through - 15 to 20 minutes.

Nutritional Information:

Calories: 311, Fat: 9g, Carbs: 31g, Protein: 25g

Air Fryer Beef Empanadas

Preparation Time: 15 minutes | Yield: 4 Servings

Ingredients:

- 8 Goya empanada discs, thawed
- 1 cup picadillo
- 1 egg white, whisked
- 1 teaspoon water

Directions:

Preheat the air fryer to 325F for 8 minutes. Spray the basket generously with cooking spray. Place 2 tbsp of picadillo in the center of each disc. Fold in half and use a fork to seal the edges. Repeat with the remaining dough. Whisk the egg whites with water, then brush the tops of the empanadas. Bake 2 or 3 at a time in the air fryer 8 minutes, or until golden. Remove from heat and repeat with the remaining empanadas.

Nutritional Information:

Calories: 183, Fat: 5g, Carbs: 22g, Protein: 11g

Air-Fried Turkey Breast with Maple Mustard Glaze

Preparation Time: 35 minutes | Yield: 4 Servings

Ingredients:

- 2 teaspoons olive oil
- 5-pound whole turkey breast
- 1 teaspoon dried thyme
- ½ teaspoon dried sage
- ½ teaspoon smoked paprika
- 1 teaspoon salt
- ½ teaspoon freshly ground black pepper
- ¼ cup maple syrup
- 2 tablespoon Dijon mustard
- 1 tablespoon butter

Directions:

Pre heat air fryer to 350°F. Brush the olive oil all over the turkey breast. Combine the thyme, sage, paprika, salt and pepper and rub the outside of the turkey breast with the spice mixture. Transfer the seasoned turkey breast to the air fryer basket and air-fry at 350°F for 25 minutes. Turn the turkey breast on its side and air-fry for another 12 minutes. Turn the turkey breast on the opposite side and air-fry for another 12 minutes. The internal temperature of the turkey breast should reach 165°F when fully cooked. While the turkey is air-frying, combine the maple syrup, mustard and butter in a small saucepan. When the cooking time is up, return the turkey breast to an upright position and brush the glaze all over the turkey. Air-fry for a final 5 minutes, until the skin is nicely browned and crispy. Let the turkey rest, loosely tented with foil, for at least 5 minutes before slicing and serving.

Nutritional Information:

Calories: 183, Fat: 5g, Carbs: 22g, Protein: 11g

Crispy Boneless Breaded Pork Chops

Preparation Time: 15 minutes | Yield: 4 Servings

Ingredients:

- 6 (3/4-inch thick) center cut boneless pork chops, fat trimmed (5 oz each)
- kosher salt
- 2 tbsp grated parmesan cheese (omit for vegetarian)
- 1 1/4 tsp sweet paprika

- 1 large egg, beaten
- 1/2 cup panko crumbs
- 1/3 cup crushed cornflakes crumbs
- 1/2 tsp garlic powder
- 1/2 tsp onion powder
- 1/4 tsp chili powder
- 1/8 tsp black pepper

Directions:

Preheat the air fryer to 400F for 12 minutes and lightly spray the basket with oil. Season pork chops on both sides with 1/2 tsp kosher salt. Combine panko, cornflake crumbs, parmesan cheese, 3/4 tsp kosher salt, paprika, garlic powder, onion powder, chili powder and black pepper in a large shallow bowl. Place the beaten egg in another. Dip the pork into the egg, then crumb mixture. When the air fryer is ready, place 3 of the chops into the prepared basket and spritz the top with oil. Cook 12 minutes turning half way, spritzing both sides with oil. Set aside and repeat with the remaining.

Nutritional Information:

Calories: 378, Fat: 13g, Carbs: 8g, Protein: 33g

Turkey Breast with Cherry Glaze

Preparation Time: 15 minutes | Yield: 4 Servings

Ingredients:

- 1 (5-pound) turkey breast
- 2 teaspoons olive oil
- 1 teaspoon dried thyme
- ½ teaspoon dried sage
- 1 teaspoon salt
- ½ teaspoon freshly ground black pepper
- ½ cup cherry preserve
- 1 tablespoon chopped fresh thyme leaves
- 1 teaspoon soy sauce
- freshly ground black pepper

Directions:

Pre-heat the air fryer to 350°F. Brush the turkey breast all over with the olive oil. Combine the thyme, sage, salt and pepper and rub the outside of the turkey breast with the spice mixture. Transfer the seasoned turkey breast to the air fryer basket, breast side up, and air-fry at 350°F for 25 minutes. Turn the turkey breast on its side and air-fry for another 12 minutes. Turn the turkey breast on the opposite side and air-fry for another 12 minutes. The internal temperature of the turkey breast should reach 165°F when fully cooked. While the turkey is air-frying, combine the cherry preserve, fresh thyme, soy sauce and pepper in a small bowl. When the cooking time is up, return the turkey breast to an upright position and brush the glaze all over the turkey. Air-fry for a final 5 minutes, until the skin is nicely browned and crispy. Let the turkey rest before serving.

Nutritional Information:

Calories: 167, Fat: 6g, Carbs: 1g, Protein: 25g

Air Fryer Coffee & Spice Ribeye

Preparation Time: 15 minutes | Yield: 4 Servings

Ingredients:

- 1 lb. ribeye steak
- 1 1/2 tsp. course sea salt
- 1 tsp. brown sugar
- 1/2 tsp. ground coffee
- 1/2 tsp. black pepper
- 1/4 tsp. chili powder

- 1/4 tsp. onion powder
- 1/4 tsp. paprika
- 1/4 tsp. chipotle powder
- 1/8 tsp. Coriander
- 1/8 tsp. cocoa powder
- 1/4 tsp. garlic powder

Directions:

In a small bowl – add all spices. Using a whisk – combine spices, making sure to break up the brown sugar. Sprinkle a generous amount of spice mix onto a plate. Lay one steak on top of spices. Then season steak liberally with spice mix and rub into meat evenly. Flip to make sure other side is seasoned properly as well. Pick up steak and press all sides into remaining spice mix on the plate so that none of the spices are wasted. Let steak sit for at least 20 minutes to come to room temperature. This helps the steak to cook evenly. Meanwhile - Prepare the air fryer tray by coating with oil to prevent sticking. Preheat air fryer to 390 degrees for at least 3 minutes. Cook steak undisturbed for 9 minutes. Do not flip and do not open. Once cooking time is finished, remove from air fryer and let rest for at least 5 minutes before slicing.

Nutritional Information:

Calories: 495, Fat: 32g, Carbs: 5g, Protein: 46g

Air Fried Meatloaf

Preparation Time: 25 minutes | Yield: 4 Servings

Ingredients:

- 1 pound lean ground beef
- 1 egg, lightly beaten
- 3 tablespoons dry bread crumbs
- 1 small onion, finely chopped
- 1 tablespoon chopped fresh thyme
- 1 teaspoon saltground black pepper to taste
- 2 mushrooms, thickly sliced
- 1 tablespoon olive oil, or as needed

Directions:

Preheat an air fryer to 392 degrees F (200 degrees C). Combine ground beef, egg, bread crumbs, onion, thyme, salt, and pepper in a bowl. Knead and mix thoroughly. Transfer beef mixture to a baking pan and smooth the top. Press mushrooms into the top and coat with olive oil. Place the pan into the air fryer basket and slide into the air fryer. Set air fryer timer for 25 minutes and roast meatloaf until nicely browned. Let meatloaf rest at least 10 minutes before slicing into wedges and serving.

Nutritional Information:

Calories: 297, Fat: 19g, Carbs: 6g, Protein: 24g

Air Fryer Chinese Salt and Pepper Pork Chops

Preparation Time: 15 minutes | Yield: 2 Servings

Ingredients:

Pork Chops:

- 1 Egg White
- 1/2 teaspoon Sea Salt
- 1/4 teaspoon Freshly Ground Black Pepper
- 3/4 cup Potato Starch (or cornstarch)
- 1 Oil Mister

Stir Fry:

- 2 Jalapeño Pepper stems removed, sliced
- 2 Scallions (Green Onions) trimmes, sliced
- 2 Tablespoons Canola Oil (or peanut)
- 1 teaspoon Sea Salt
- 1/4 teaspoon Freshly Ground Black Pepper
- Cast Iron Chicken Fryer

Directions:

Coat Air Fryer Basket with a thin coat of Oil. In a medium bowl, whisk together egg white, salt and pepper until foamy. Slice pork chops into cutlet pieces, leaving a little on the bones and pat dry. Add pork chop pieces to egg white mixture. Coat thoroughly. Marinate for at least 20 minutes. Transfer pork chops into a large bowl and add Potato Starch. Dredge the pork chops through the Potato Starch thoroughly. Shake off pork and place into a prepared Air Fryer Basket. Lightly spray pork with oil. Cook at 360 degrees for 9 minutes, shaking the basket often and spraying with oil between shakes. Cook an additional 6 minutes at 400 degrees, or until the pork is brown and crispy.

Stir Fry:

Slice Jalapeños thin and remove seeds. Chop scallions. Place in bowl and set aside. Heat wok or skillet until screaming hot. Add oil, Jalapeño peppers, Scallions, salt and pepper and stir fry for about a minute. Add air fried pork pieces to the wok or skillet and toss them with the Jalapeño and Scallions. Stir Fry pork for another minute, making sure they become coated with the hot oil and vegetables.

Nutritional Information:

Calories: 305, Fat: 13g, Carbs: 1g, Protein: 24g

Air Fryer Country Fried Steak

Preparation Time: 15 minutes | Yield: 4 Servings

Ingredients:

- 6 ounce sirloin steak-pounded thin
- 3 eggs, beaten
- 1 cup flour
- 1 cup Panko
- 1 teaspoon onion powder
- 1 teaspoon garlic powder
- 1 teaspoon salt
- 1 teaspoon pepper
- 6 ounce ground sausage meat
- 2 tablespoon flour
- 2 cup milk
- 1 teaspoon pepper

Directions:

Season the panko with the spices. Dredge the steak in this order: flour, egg, and seasoned panko. Place the breaded steak into the basket of the Air Fryer and close. Press the M button the Defaut temperature of 370 F and set the time for 12 minutes. Press the power button. Once the timer has elapsed remove the steak and serve with mash potatoes and sausage gravy.

Sausage Gravy:

In a pan cook the sausage until well done. Drain fat, reserve 2 tbsp in the pan. Add in the flour to the pan with sausage, mix until all the flour is incorporated. Slowly mix in the milk. Stir over a med heat until the milk thickens. Season with pepper. Cook for 3 minutes to cook out the flour.

Nutritional Information:

Calories: 311, Fat: 15g, Carbs: 15g, Protein: 25g

Air Fryer Italian-Style Meatballs

Preparation Time: 45 minutes | Yield: 12 Servings

Ingredients:

- 2 tablespoons olive oil
- 1 medium shallot, minced (about 2 Tbsp.)
- 3 cloves garlic, minced (about 1 Tbsp.)
- 1/4 cup whole-wheat panko crumbs
- 2 tablespoons whole milk
- 2/3 pound lean ground beef
- 1/3 pound bulk turkey sausage

- 1 large egg, lightly beaten
- 1/4 cup finely chopped fresh flat-leaf parsley
- 1 tablespoon finely chopped fresh rosemary
- 1 tablespoon finely chopped fresh thyme
- 1 tablespoon Dijon mustard
- 1/2 teaspoon kosher salt

Directions:

Preheat air-fryer to 400°F. Heat oil in a medium nonstick pan over medium-high heat. Add shallot and cook until softened, 1 to 2 minutes. Add garlic and cook just until fragrant, 1 minute. Remove from heat. In a large bowl, combine panko and milk. Let stand 5 minutes. Add cooked shallot and garlic to panko mixture, along with beef, turkey sausage egg, parsley, rosemary, thyme, mustard, and salt. Stir to gently combine. Gently shape mixture into 1 1/2-inch balls. Place shaped balls in a single-layer in air-fryer basket. Cook half the meatballs at 400°F until lightly browned and cooked-through, 10 to 11 minutes. Remove and keep warm. Repeat with remaining meatballs. Serve warm meatballs with toothpicks as an appetizer or serve over pasta, rice, or spiralized zoodles for a main dish.

Nutritional Information:

Calories: 122, Fat: 8g, Carbs: 0g, Protein: 10g

Air Fried Pork Chops With Brussels Sprouts

Preparation Time: 25 minutes | Yield: 2 Servings

Ingredients:

- 8 ounces bone-in center-cut pork chop
- Cooking spray
- 1/8 teaspoon kosher salt
- 1/2 teaspoon black pepper, divided

- 1 teaspoon pure maple syrup
- 1 teaspoon Dijon mustard
- 6 ounces Brussels sprouts, quartered
- 1 teaspoon olive oil

Directions:

Lightly coat pork chop with cooking spray; sprinkle with salt and 1/4 teaspoon of the pepper. Whisk together oil, syrup, mustard, and remaining 1/4 teaspoon pepper in a medium bowl; add Brussels sprouts; toss to coat. Place pork chop on 1 side of air fryer basket, and coated Brussels sprouts on other side. Heat air fryer to 400°F, and cook until golden brown and pork is cooked to desired temperature, about 10 minutes for medium or 13 minutes for well-done.

Nutritional Information:

Calories: 377, Fat: 11g, Carbs: 21g, Protein: 40g

Thanksgiving Turkey

Preparation Time: 35 minutes | Yield: 4 Servings

Ingredients:

- 1 (2-lb.) turkey breast

- 1 tsp. freshly chopped sage

- Kosher salt
- Freshly ground black pepper
- 1 tsp. freshly chopped thyme
- 1 tsp. freshly chopped rosemary
- 1/4 c. maple syrup
- 2 tbsp. dijon mustard
- 1 tbsp. butter, melted

Directions:

Season turkey breast generously with salt and pepper, then rub all over with fresh herbs. Place in air fryer and fry at 390° for 30 to 35 minutes or until the internal temperature reaches 160°. In a small bowl, whisk together maple syrup, dijon, and melted butter. Remove turkey from air fryer and brush mixture all over. Return to air fryer and fry at 330° until caramelized, 2 minutes. Let rest 15 minutes before slicing.

Nutritional Information:

Calories: 167, Fat: 7g, Carbs: 1g, Protein: 25g

Ultimate Air Fryer Burgers

Preparation Time: 45 minutes | Yield: 4 Servings

Ingredients:

- 300 g Mixed Mince pork and beef
- Onion
- 1 Tsp Garlic Puree
- 1 Tsp Tomato Puree
- 1 Tsp Mustard
- 1 Tsp Basil
- 1 Tsp Mixed Herbs
- Salt & Pepper
- 25 g Cheddar Cheese
- 4 Bread Buns
- Salad for burger topping

Directions:

In a mixing bowl add the mince and seasoning and mix well. Form into four medium sized burgers and place in the Air Fryer cooking tray. Cook in the Air Fryer on 200c for 25 minutes and then check on them and then cook them for further 20 minutes on 180c. Then add your salad, cheese and bun and serve!

Nutritional Information:

Calories: 344, Fat: 19g, Carbs: 22g, Protein: 19g

Perfect Air Fryer Steak with Garlic Herb Butter

Preparation Time: 15 minutes | Yield: 2 Servings

Ingredients:

- 2 - 8 oz Ribeye steak
- salt
- freshly cracked black pepper
- olive oil
- Garlic Butter

- 2 Tbsp fresh parsley chopped
- 2 tsp garlic minced
- 1 tsp Worcestershire Sauce
- 1/2 tsp salt
- 1 stick unsalted butter softened

Directions:

Prepare Garlic Butter by mixing butter, parsley garlic, worcestershire sauce, and salt until thoroughly combined. Place in parchment paper and roll into a log. Refrigerate until ready to use. Remove steak from fridge and allow to sit at room temperature for 20 minutes. Rub a little bit of olive oil on both side of the steak and season with salt and freshly cracked black pepper. Grease your Air Fryer basket by rubbing a little bit of oil on the basket. Preheat Air Fryer to 400 degrees Fahrenheit. Once preheated, place steaks in air fryer and cook for 12 minutes, flipping halfway through. Remove from air fryer and allow to rest for 5 minutes. Top with garlic butter.

Nutritional Information:

Calories: 683, Fat: 24g, Carbs: 22g, Protein: 25g

Air Fryer Mongolian Beef

Preparation Time: 25 minutes | Yield: 4 Servings

Ingredients:

Meat

- 1 Lb Flank Steak
- 1/4 Cup Corn Starch

Sauce

- 2 Tsp Vegetable Oil
- 1/2 Tsp Ginger
- 1 Tbsp Minced Garlic
- 1/2 Cup Soy Sauce or Gluten Free Soy Sauce
- 1/2 Cup Water
- 3/4 Cup Brown Sugar Packed

Directions:

Thinly slice the steak in long pieces, then coat with the corn starch. Place in the Air Fryer and cook on 390 for 10 minutes on each side. While the steak cooks, warm up all sauce ingredient in a medium sized saucepan on medium-high heat. Whisk the ingredients together until it gets to a low boil. Once both the steak and sauce are cooked, place the steak in a bowl with the sauce and let it soak in for about 5-10 minutes. When ready to serve, use tongs to remove the steak and let the excess sauce drip off. Place steak on cooked rice and green beans, top with additional sauce if you prefer.

Nutritional Information:

Calories: 258, Fat: 11g, Carbs: 8g, Protein: 30g

Air Fryer Beef Stir Fry With Homemade Marinade

Preparation Time: 15 minutes | Yield: 4 Servings

Ingredients:

- 1 pound of beef sirloin, cut into 2 inch strips
- 1½ pounds of broccoli florets
- 1 red pepper, cut into strips
- 1 yellow pepper, cut into strips
- ½ cup of onion, cut into strips
- ½ cup of red onion, cut into strips
- 1 green pepper, cut into strips

Sauce/Marinade:

- ¼ cup of hoisin sauce
- 2 teaspoons of minced garlic
- 1 teaspoon of sesame oil
- 1 tablespoon of soy sauce
- 1 teaspoon of ground ginger
- ¼ cup of water

Directions:

Add all of the ingredients for the sauce (marinate) to a bowl, then add the meat. Then place in the refrigerator for about 20 minutes. Add one tablespoon of stir fryer oil, and mix it in with the vegetables. Place your vegetables in the air fryer basket, and cook them for about 5 minutes on 200 degrees F. Then open your air fryer, mix all of the vegetables, and make sure they are softened, not hard. If they aren't softened, add another 2 minutes. Remove the vegetables and place them in a bowl, then add your meat to the air fryer basket, and cook them for 4 minutes at 360. Check and flip them, and do another 2 minutes if they aren't done. I served my stir fry over white rice. Then topped it with the vegetables and meat.

Nutritional Information:

Calories: 160, Fat: 6g, Carbs: 0g, Protein: 25g

Air Fryer Marinated Steak

Preparation Time: 25 minutes | Yield: 2 Servings

Ingredients:

- About 6-8 oz Strip Steaks
- 1 tablespoon low-sodium soy sauce
- 1 teaspoon liquid smoke or a cap full
- salt and pepper to taste
- melted butter (optional)

- 1 tablespoon McCormick's Grill Mates Montreal Steak Seasoning or Steak Rub (or season to taste)
- 1/2 tablespoon unsweetened cocoa powder

Directions:

Drizzle the Steak with the soy sauce and liquid smoke. You can do this inside Ziploc bags. Season the steak with the seasonings. Refrigerate for at least a couple of hours, preferably overnight. Place the steak in the air fryer. I did not use any oil. Cook two steaks at a time (if air fryer is standard size). You can use an accessory grill pan, a layer rack or the standard air fryer basket. Cook for 5 minutes on 375 degrees. After 5 minutes, open the air fryer and examine your steak. Cook time will vary depending on your desired doneness. Check the inside of the steak to determine if they have finished cooking. You can stick a knife or fork in the center to review the level of pink. You can also use a meat thermometer and cook to 125° F for rare, 135° F for medium-rare, 145° F for medium, 155° F for medium-well, and 160° F for well done. For medium steak, at 5 minutes, I flipped my steak and cooked for an additional 2 minutes, 7 minutes cook time total using the Power Air Fryer. Each air fryer brand is different and will cook at different speeds. I also have the Black + Decker Air Fryer and 5 minutes at 370 degrees was enough time to produce medium done steak. At 7 minutes, the steak was near well done. Examine your steak and do what works best for you. Remove the steak from the air fryer and drizzle with melted butter.

Nutritional Information:

Calorizs: 476, Fat: 28g, Carbs: 1g, Protein: 49g

Air Fryer Paleo Sirloin Steak

Preparation Time: 25 minutes | Yield: 4 Servings

Ingredients:

- 2 Sirloin Steaks
- 2 Tbsp. Primal Palate Steak Seasoning
- Cooking Fat (ghee, coconut oil or avocado oil)

Directions:

Preheat your air fryer for 5 minutes at 392 degrees. Remove the steak from the fridge and pat dry (preferably let it sit out until it is room temperature). Brush (or spray) the top of the sirloin with cooking fat (about 1-2 tsp.) and season generously. Coat the bottom of the air fryer basket in cooking fat and add the sirloin steak to the basket. Cook for 5 minutes. Flip the sirloin steak and cook an additional 5 minutes. Remove the steak from the air fryer and let it rest for 5 minutes before slicing and servings.

Nutritional Information:

Calories: 276, Fat: 15g, Carbs: 5g, Protein: 25g

Air Fryer Steak Fajita's

Preparation Time: 25 minutes | Yield: 4 Servings

Ingredients:

- 1.25 lbs. of Beef Steak Strips Stir Fry Cut
- 1 Red Bell Pepper julienned
- 1 teaspoon of Paprika
- 1 teaspoon of Chili Powder

- 1 Yellow Bell Pepper julienned
- 1 Green Bell Pepper julienned
- 1 Red Onion sliced
- 2 teaspoon of Garlic Powder
- 2 teaspoon of ground Cumin
- 1 teaspoon of Mexican Oregano
- 1 teaspoon of Salt
- 2 tablespoon of Salt

Directions:

In a small bowl, combine the garlic powder, paprika, chili powder, cumin, oregano and salt. Mix it well. In a large bowl, combine the julienned peppers, sliced onion and the beef strips. Place the prepared spice blend in with the oil. Give everything a good mix, making sure the beef and the peppers are well coated in oil and the spice blend. Divide the mix into two batches. Spread one batch of the beef and vegetables in a well-greased air fryer basket. Air fry at 390 F for 10 minutes. Repeat with the other batch. Serve hot in a warmed white or yellow corn tortilla and your favorite add-ins and a squeeze of lime juice.

Nutritional Information:

Calories: 329, Fat: 18g, Carbs: 5g, Protein: 32g

Keto Meat Recipes

Air Fryer Steak with Garlic Butter

Preparation Time: 25 minutes | Yield: 2 Servings

Ingredients:

- 2 8 oz Ribeye steak
- salt
- freshly cracked black pepper
- 1 stick unsalted butter softened
- olive oil

Garlic Butter
- 1 stick unsalted butter softened
- 2 Tbsp fresh parsley chopped
- 2 tsp garlic minced
- 1 tsp Worcestershire Sauce
- 1/2 tsp salt

Directions:

Prepare Garlic Butter by mixing butter, parsley garlic, worcestershire sauce, and salt until thoroughly combined. Place in parchment paper and roll into a log. Refrigerate until ready to use. Remove steak from fridge and allow to sit at room temperature for 20 minutes. Rub a little bit of olive oil on both side of the steak and season with salt and freshly cracked black pepper. Grease your Air Fryer basket by rubbing a little bit of oil on the basket. Preheat Air Fryer to 400 degrees Fahrenheit. Once preheated, place steaks in air fryer and cook for 12 minutes, flipping halfway through. Remove from air fryer and allow to rest for 5 minutes. Top with garlic butter.

Nutritional Information:

Calories: 253, Fat: 11G, Carbs: 9g, Protein: 26g

Air Fryer Meatloaf

Preparation Time: 25 minutes | Yield: 4 Servings

Ingredients:

- 1 cup pork rind panko breadcrumbs
- ¼ cup beef broth
- ½ cup chopped mushrooms
- ½ cup shredded carrots
- ½ cup chopped onions
- 2 cloves garlic
- 2 eggs lightly beaten
- 1 Tbsp Dijon style mustard
- 1 Tbsp Worcestershire sauce
- ½ tsp kosher salt
- 2lbs ground beef

For glaze
- ½ cup Heinz No Sugar Added Ketchup
- ¼ cup granulated erythritol sweetener
- 2 tsp dijon mustard

Directions:

Add pork rind panko breadcrumbs and beef broth to a small bowl and stir until breadcrumbs are coated. Set aside. Add mushrooms, carrots, onions, and garlic and process until finely chopped. Place in large bowl. Add ground beef, soaked breadcrumbs, Dijon style mustard, Worcestershire sauce, and salt to large bowl. Mix with hands until incorporated. Form into a loaf. Preheat Air Fryer to 390 degrees. Place meatloaf in Air Fryer and cook for 40-45 minutes. While meatloaf is cooking, prepare glaze by combining ketchup, granulated erythritol sweetener, and dijon mustard. When there are about 5 minutes left on your timer, spread glaze over meatloaf in Air Fryer. Remove and allow meatloaf to rest for 10 minutes before slicing.

Nutritional Information:

Calories: 407, Fat: 15G, Carbs: 9g, Protein: 30g

Air Fryer Ribeye with Coffee and Spice

Preparation Time: 35 minutes | Yield: 4 Servings

Ingredients:

- 1 lb. ribeye steak
- 1 1/2 tsp. course sea salt
- 1 tsp. ranulated erythritol sweetener
- 1/2 tsp. ground coffee
- 1/2 tsp. black pepper
- 1/4 tsp. chili powder
- 1/4 tsp. garlic powder
- 1/4 tsp. onion powder
- 1/4 tsp. paprika
- 1/4 tsp. chipotle powder
- 1/8 tsp. Coriander
- 1/8 tsp. cocoa powder

Directions:

In a small bowl – add all spices. Using a whisk – combine spices, making sure to break up the brown sugar. Sprinkle a generous amount of spice mix onto a plate. Lay one steak on top of spices. Then season steak liberally with spice mix and rub into meat evenly. Flip to make sure other side is seasoned properly as well. Pick up steak and press all sides into remaining spice mix on the plate so that none of the spices are wasted. Let steak sit for at least 20 minutes to come to room temperature. This helps the steak cook evenly. Meanwhile – Prepare the air fryer tray by coating with oil to prevent sticking. Preheat air fryer to 390 degrees for at least 3 minutes. Cook steak undisturbed for 9 minutes. Do not flip and do not open. Once cook time is finished, remove from air fryer and let rest for at least 5 minutes before slicing.

Nutritional Information:

Calories: 495, Fat: 32G, Carbs: 5g, Protein: 46g

Air Fryer Crispy Pork Belly

Preparation Time: 25 minutes | Yield: 4 Servings

Ingredients:

- 1 pound pork belly
- 3 cups water
- 1 teaspoon salt
- 1 teaspoon pepper
- 2 tablespoons soy sauce
- 2 bay leaves
- 6 cloves garlic

Directions:

Cut the pork belly into 3 thick chunks so that it cooks more evenly. Place all ingredients into the inner liner of an Instant Pot or pressure cooker. Cook the pork belly at high pressure for 15 minutes. Allow the pot to sit undisturbed for 10 minutes and then release all remaining pressure. Using a set of tongs, very carefully remove the meat from the pressure cooker. Allow the meat to drain and dry for 10 minutes. If you do not have a pressure cooker, place the ingredients into a sauce pan, cover, and cook for 60 minutes, until a knife can be easily inserted into the skin-side of the pork belly. Remove the meat and allow the meat to drain and dry for 10 minutes. Cut each of the three chunks of pork belly into 2 long slices. Place the pork belly slices in the air fryer basket. Set the air fryer to 400°F for 15 minutes or until the fat on the pork belly has crisped up, and then serve.

Nutritional Information:

Calories: 594, Fat: 30g, Carbs: 2G, Protein: 11g

Keto Beef Satay

Preparation Time: 25 minutes | Yield: 4 Servings

Ingredients:

- 1 pound beef flank steak sliced thinly into long strips
- 2 tablespoons oil
- 1 tablespoon fish sauce
- 1 tablespoon soy sauce
- 1 tablespoon minced ginger
- 1 tablespoon sugar
- 1 teaspoon Sriracha or other hot sauce
- 1 teaspoon ground coriander
- 1/2 cup chopped cilantro divided
- 1/4 cup chopped roasted peanuts
- 1 tablespoon minced garlic

Directions:

Place beef strips into a large bowl or a ziplock bag. Add oil, fish sauce, soy sauce, ginger, garlic, sugar, Sriracha, coriander, and 1/4 cup cilantro to the beef and mix well. Marinate for 30 minutes or up to 24 hours in the refrigerator. Using a set of tongs, place the beef strips in the air fryer basket, laying them side by side and minimizing overlap. Leave behind as much of the marinade as you can and discard this marinade. Set your air fryer to 400F for 8 minutes, flipping once halfway. Remove the meat to a serving tray, top with remaining 1/4 cup chopped cilantro and the chopped roasted peanuts. Serve with Easy Peanut Sauce.

Nutritional Information:

Calories: 594, Fat: 30g, Carbs: 2G, Protein: 11g

Air Fryer Bacon

Preparation Time: 10 minutes | Yield: 11 Servings

Ingredients:

- 11 slices bacon, thick cut

Directions:

Divide the bacon in half, and place the first half in the air fryer. Set the temperature at 400 degrees, and set the timer to 10 minutes (possibly less time for thinner bacon). Check it halfway through to see if anything needs to be rearranged (tongs are helpful!). Cook remainder of the time. Check for desired doneness.

Nutritional Information:

Calories: 91, Fat: 8g, Carbs: 0g, Protein: 2G

Keto Air Fryer Meatloaf Sliders

Preparation Time: 25 minutes | Yield: 8 Servings

Ingredients:

- 1 lb ground beef 80/20 fat
- 2 eggs beaten
- ¼ C onion finely chopped
- 1 clove garlic minced
- ½ C blanched almond flour extra fine
- ¼ C coconut flour
- ¼ C ketchup
- ½ tsp sea salt
- ½ tsp black pepper
- 1 Tbsp Worcestershire Sauce
- 1 tsp Italian Seasoning See below
- ½ tsp Tarragon dried

Directions:

In a large mixing bowl, combine all the ingredients and mix well. Make patties that are about 2" in diameter and about 1" thick. If you want to make thicker or thinner patties, make sure all of them are similar in size, so they cook properly at the same time. Place the patties on a platter and refrigerate for 10 minutes for the flour to absorb the wet ingredients and the patties to become firm. Preheat the air fryer to 360°F. Place as many patties you can fit in the basket and close. Set the timer for 10 minutes. Check the patties half way. When the timer goes off, take them out to a serving platter and cover until all the patties are cooked. These sliders are perfect on your favorite paleo breads or biscuits (P.164) or on lettuce wraps or with a side of spring greens.

Nutritional Information:

Calories: 228, Fat: 16G, Carbs: 6g, Protein: 13g

Air Fried Spicy Bacon Bites

Preparation Time: 15 minutes | Yield: 4 Servings

Ingredients:

- 4 strips of bacon
- 1/4 cup hot sauce
- 1/2 cup crushed pork rinds

Directions:

Cut uncooked bacon slices into 6 even pieces and place in a bowl. Add hot sauce to bowl, ensuring both sides of bacon get sauce. Dip bacon pieces into crushed pork rinds, coating both sides. Cook in air fryer on 350F for 10 minutes, checking around 8 minutes to ensure it's not burning.

Nutritional Information:

Calories: 120, Fat: 8g, Carbs: 0g, Protein: 7g

Keto Lasagna

Preparation Time: 30 minutes | Yield: 4 Servings

Ingredients:

- 1 cup marinara sauce
- 1 zucchini sliced into long thin sliced

For Meat Layer

- 1 cup diced yellow or white onion
- 1 teaspoon minced garlic
- 1/2 pound bulk hot or mild Italian sausageFor Cheese Layer (mix all
- 1/2 cup shredded mozzarella cheese
- 1/2 cup shredded parmesan, divided
- 1 egg
- 1/2 teaspoon garlic minced

ingredients together in a bowl)
- 1/2 cup ricotta cheese

- 1/2 teaspoon dried Italian seasoning
- 1/2 teaspoon black pepper

Directions:

Using a mandolin, slice the zucchini into long, thin slices. Spray a 7-inch springform pan with oil and arrange the zucchini in overlapping layers in the bottom of the pan. Place 1/4 cup of marinara sauce on top of the zucchini and spread evenly. In a large bowl, mix the onions, garlic, and Italian sausage. Layer the meat on top of the zucchini and spread evenly. Pour the rest of the marinara sauce and spread it evenly. Rinse the bowl you used earlier, and mix together the ricotta and mozzarella and 1/4 of a cup of the Parmesan cheese. Spread the cheese mixture on top of the meat. Top with the remaining 1/4 cup parmesan cheese. To recap, the layer are so: zucchini, sauce, meat, sauce, cheese mix, parmesan cheese. Cover the pan with foil or a silicone lid. Set the air fryer to 350F and bake for 20 minutes. Then, remove the foil and cook for another 8-10 minutes at 350F until the top is browned and bubbling. Allow the lasagna to rest for 10 minutes before unclasping the springform pan to serve.

Nutritional Information:

Calories: 375, Fat: 27G, Carbs: 8g, Protein: 17g

Rib Eye Steak with Blue Cheese Butter

Preparation Time: 25 minutes | Yield: 4 Servings

Ingredients:

- 2 12 - 16 ounce Rib Eye Steaks 1 inch thick (or larger)
- 2 teaspoons Kosher Salt

- 1.5 teaspoon Freshly Ground Black Pepper
- 1 teaspoon Garlic Powder
- 2 Tablespoons Blue Cheese Butter

Directions:

Remove rib eye steaks from refrigerator 15 minutes before starting recipe. Turn air fryer to 400 degrees (or the highest temp possible) and set time to 15 minutes. Air fryer needs to preheat at least 5 minutes before place in steaks. Coat both sides of steaks with salt, garlic powder and pepper. With your hand, press seasonings into steaks. Open air fryer and quickly place both steaks into basket and close. Cook at 400 degrees for 4 minutes and then quickly flip steaks over and cook for 3 minutes more. Turn off air fryer and do not open. Let sit for 1 minute for rare. For medium rare, let sit 2 minutes. For less rare 3 minutes, and so on. Top with Blue Cheese Butter.

Nutritional Information:

Calories: 829, Fat: 60g, Carbs: 2G, Protein: 70g

Bacon Wrapped Filet Mignon

Preparation Time: 25 minutes | Yield: 4 Servings

Ingredients:

- 2 filet mignon steaks
- 2 slices of bacon
- 2 toothpicks
- avocado oil

- 1 teaspoon freshly cracked peppercorns we use a variety of peppercorns
- 1/2 teaspoon kosher salt

Directions:

Wrap the bacon around the filet mignon and secure with a toothpick by pressing the toothpick through the bacon and into the filet, then out of the filet into the bacon on the other end of the toothpick. Season the steak with the salt and pepper or your favorite seasonings. Place the bacon wrapped filet mignon onto your air fryer rack. Spray a little avocado oil onto the steak. How long to cook bacon wrapped filet mignon Air fry the steak for about 10 minutes on 375 degrees F and then flip as one side will be nice and seared while the other isn't. Air fry for another 5 minutes or until you reach the desired doneness. We're aiming for medium.

Nutritional Information:

Calories: 557, Fat: 26G, Carbs: 1G, Protein: 29g

Crispy Fried Pork Chops

Preparation Time: 15 minutes | Yield: 4 Servings

Ingredients:

- 1 1/2 lb boneless pork chops
- 1/3 cup Almond Flour
- 1/4 cup grated Parmesan cheese
- 1 tsp garlic powder
- 1 tsp Tony Chachere's Creole Seasoning
- 1 tsp Paprika

Directions:

Preheat your air fryer to 360 degrees F. Meanwhile, combine all ingredients EXCEPT pork chops into a large ziplock bag. Place the pork chops into the bag, seal it, and then shake to coat the pork chops. Remove from the bag and place in the air fryer in a single layer. Cook for 8-12 minutes depending upon the thickness of your pork chops.

Nutritional Information:

Calories: 222, Fat: 11G, Carbs: 2G, Protein: 26g

Air Fryer Hamburgers

Preparation Time: 15 minutes | Yield: 4 Servings

Ingredients:

- 1 pound ground beef lean
- salt & pepper to taste

Directions:

Preheat Air Fryer on 400 degrees F for 2-3 minutes. Divide ground beef into 4 even portions and form into round patties. Season both sides to taste. Place hamburger patties in a single layer in the basket of Air Fryer. Cook on 400 degrees F for 10 minutes. Flip patties then cook another 2-3 minutes until fully cooked.

Nutritional Information:

Calories: 148, Fat: 4g, Carbs: 0g, Protein: 24g

Parmesan Meatballs

Preparation Time: 25 minutes | Yield: 4 Servings

Ingredients:

- 2 pounds ground beef
- 1/4 cup parmesan cheese, grated
- 1/3 cup pork rind panko breadcrumbs
- 3 tablespoons chopped fresh Italian parsley
- 1/4 cup dried minced onion
- 1 tablespoon Worcestershire sauce
- 2 eggs
- salt & pepper to taste
- 1 teaspoon minced garlic

Directions:

Prep air fryer by greasing the inner basket. In a large mixing bowl, combine all meatball ingredients and mix well using a potato masher. Roll 2-inch sized meatballs and place in a single layer in the air fryer, without them touching. I'm able to fit about 12-14 in my 6-quart air fryer at a time. Cook at 350 degrees for about 13-14 minutes. Start checking at 12 minutes to see if done, as cook times can vary a little. Optional Step: Place meatballs in a small, oven-safe dish. Drizzle with marinara sauce and a little extra cheese. Place back into the air fryer for a couple minutes to melt. Serve meatballs as desired with spaghetti and marinara, by themselves, or in a sandwich as desired.

Nutritional Information:

Calories: 64, Fat: 3g, Carbs: 1G, Protein: 5g

Air Fryer Roast Beef

Preparation Time: 45 minutes | Yield: 6 Servings

Ingredients:

- 2 lb beef roast
- 1 tbsp olive oil
- 1 tsp salt
- 1 tsp rosemary

Directions:

Preheat air fryer to 360°F (180°C). Mix sea salt, rosemary and oil on a plate. Place beef on plate and turn so that the oil-herb mix coats the outside. Place beef in air fryer basket. Set to cook in air fryer for 45 minutes. This should give you medium-rare beef. Though when cooking roast beef in an air fryer it is best to check the temperature with a meat thermometer to ensure that it is cooked to your liking. Cook for an additional 5 minute intervals if you prefer it more well done. Remove roast beef from air fryer, cover with kitchen foil and leave to rest for ten minutes before serving (this allows the juices to reabsorb into the meat).

Nutritional Information:

Calories: 320, Fat: 12G, Carbs: 2G, Protein: 15g

Chinese Style Spare Ribs

Preparation Time: 15 minutes | Yield: 4 Servings

Ingredients:

- 1 tablespoon sesame oil
- 1 teaspoon minced garlic
- 1 teaspoon minced ginger
- 1 tablespoon fermented black bean paste

- 1 tablespoon Shaoxing wine
- 1 tablespoon dark soy sauce
- 1 tablespoon agave nectar or honey
- 1.5 pounds spareribs cut into small pieces

Directions:

In a large mixing bowl, stir together all ingredients for the marinade. Add the spare ribs and mix well. Allow the ribs to marinade for at least 30 minutes or up to 24 hours. When you're ready to cook the ribs, remove the ribs from the marinade and place into the air fryer basket. Set the air fryer at 375F for 8 minutes. Check to ensure the ribs have an internal temperature of 165F before serving.

Nutritional Information:

Calories: 386, Fat: 31G, Carbs: 4g, Protein: 18g

Air Fryer Hot Dogs

Preparation Time: 15 minutes | Yield: 4 Servings

Ingredients:

- 4 hot dogs all beef

Directions:

Score the hot dogs so that they have little slits, this will make it look nice and prevent the hot dogs from bursting and enlarging in areas. Once they're slit you can place into your air fryer. Bake the hot dogs for 5 minutes at 375 degrees F. Rotate the hot dogs and cook for 3 more minutes. Remove the hot dogs once done and eat as desired.

Nutritional Information:

Calories: 112, Fat: 6g, Carbs: 8g, Protein: 4g

Keto Butter Burgers and Air Fryer Onion Straws

Preparation Time: 25 minutes | Yield: 6 Servings

Ingredients:

- 1 1/2 lb ground chuck
- salt and pepper
- 2 tablespoons butter, sliced into 6 pieces
- 1/4 cup mayo
  - oz pork rinds
- 1/2 cup parmesan cheese, grated
- 1 teaspoon paprika
- 1 teaspoon garlic powder
- 1 onion, thinly sliced
- 6 slices gouda cheese
- pickled onions and jalapeños (optional)

Directions:

Divide the meat in to six pieces. Take 1 piece and pat it down a bit and then place a teaspoon slab of butter in the middle. Fold the sides over as best you can and then flatten to a patty. Repeat with remaining meat and butter. Liberally sprinkle salt and pepper on both sides of the burgers. Heat up a large cast iron skillet and then place the burgers on it. Do not move the burgers and cook for 4-5 minutes per side. If using cheese, place on burgers after you flip them. When done let set for a few minutes. Meanwhile place sliced onions and mayo in a food bag. Squish the mayo and onions around until the onions are all covered in mayo. Add the pork rinds, parmesan cheese, paprika and garlic powder to a food processor to make the breading. Then pour them into a large shallow bowl and mix well. Take out the onions from the food bag and mix around in the pork rind coating. Carefully place the onions into the basket of the air fryer. Sprinkle with any leftover bread crumbs on to the onions. NOTE: I like to place a piece of foil under the basket to make clean up easier. Set the air fryer to 400 degrees F and cook for 5-6 minutes. Check at 5 minutes to make sure they don't burn. Place the burgers on a piece of leaf lettuce, top with pickled jalapeños and fried onions.

Nutritional Information:

Calories: 610, Fat: 26G, Carbs: 7g, Protein: 35g

Air Fryer Juicy Beef Kabobs

Preparation Time: 10 minutes | Yield: 4 Servings

Ingredients:

- 1 lb beef chuck ribs cut in 1 inch pieces or any other tender cut meat- think nice steak, stew meat
- 1/3 cup low fat sour cream

- 2 tbsp soy sauce
- 8 6 inch skewers
- 1 bell peppers
- 1/2 onion

Directions:

Mix sour cream with soy sauce in a medium bowl. Place beef chunks into the bowl and marinate for at least 30 minuteso better overnight. Cut bell pepper and onion in 1 inch pieces. Soak wooden skewers in water for about 10 minutes. Thread beef, onions and bell peppers onto skewers. Add some freshly gound black pepper. Cook in preheated to 400F Air fryer for 10 minutes, turning half way.

Nutritional Information:

Calories: 250, Fat: 15G, Carbs: 4g, Protein: 23g

Turkey Breast with Herb Butter

Preparation Time: 25 minutes | Yield: 6 Servings

Ingredients:

- 1 (5- to 6-pound) whole turkey breast, rib bones trimmed
- ½ cup unsalted butter, room temperature
- 1 tablespoon chopped fresh parsley
- 1 tablespoon chopped fresh sage

- 1 tablespoon chopped fresh rosemary
- 1 tablespoon chopped fresh thyme
- 1 teaspoon salt
- ½ teaspoon freshly ground black pepper

Gravy (optional):

- 2 tablespoons butter
- 2 tablespoons all-purpose flour
- ¼ cup brandy or white wine
- 1½ cups rich turkey (or chicken) stock

- salt and freshly ground black pepper, to taste
- a few dashes of Worcestershire sauce
- drippings from the roast turkey

Directions:

Start by making sure the turkey breast will fit into your air fryer. Trim the rib bones with a pair of sharp poultry scissors if necessary to make sure the turkey will fit nicely and not sit higher than the top of the basket. Combine the butter, chopped fresh herbs, salt and freshly ground black pepper in a small bowl. Gently slide your fingers underneath the skin of the turkey to loosen the skin away from both sides of the turkey breast. Place a third of the herb butter under the skin, massaging it over the turkey breast. Repeat with the other side. Melt the remaining herb butter in a small saucepan (or in the microwave) and brush it all over the skin of the turkey breast, or flatten the butter with your hands and let it rest on top of the turkey. Pre-heat the air fryer to 350°F. Place the turkey breast skin-side up in the air fryer basket. Air-fry for 20 minutes at 350°F. Turn the turkey breast over so that it is now skin-side down. Use a turkey baster to suck up some of the juices from the bottom drawer and baste the turkey breast with the drippings. Air-fry for another 20 minutes. While the turkey is air-frying, make the gravy on the stovetop if you choose to do so. Pre-heat a 2-quart saucepan over medium heat. Add the butter and let it melt. Add the flour and whisk the butter and flour together, cooking for about 2 minutes. Add the brandy or white wine and let it bubble and thicken. Then, whisk in the stock, continuing to whisk until the mixture comes to a boil and thickens. Season with salt, freshly ground black pepper and the Worcestershire sauce and then set the gravy aside. Turn the turkey breast back over so that it is once again skin-side up. Baste again with the juices from the bottom of the air fryer drawer and air-fry for another 10 minutes, until the skin is crispy and the turkey reaches an internal temperature of 165°F on an instant read thermometer. Place the turkey breast on cutting board and let it rest for at least 15 minutes before carving. While the turkey rests, pour the juices from the bottom of the air fryer into a measuring cup or fat separator. Let the juices sit for 10 minutes and ladle or pour off the grease that rises to the surface. Strain the drippings and either add them to the gravy or just pour the juices over the sliced turkey breast.

Nutritional Information:

Calories: 150, Fat: 8g, Carbs: 2G, Protein: 12g

Vegetable Recipes

Air Fryer Fried Ravioli

Preparation Time: 10 minutes | Yield: 6 Servings

Ingredients:

- 1 (14-ounce) jar marinara sauce
- 1 (9-ounce) box cheese ravioli, store-bought or meat ravioli
- 1 teaspoon olive oil
- 2 cups Italian-style bread crumbs
- 1 cup buttermilk
- 1/4 cup Parmesan cheese

Directions:

Dip ravioli in buttermilk. Add olive oil to breadcrumbs, then press the ravioli into it. Put breaded ravioli into heated airfryer on baking paper and cook at 200°F for about 5 minutes. Serve warm with marinara sauce for dipping.

Nutritional Information:

Calories: 319, Fat: 12g, Carbs: 52g, Protein: 17g

Spicy Cauliflower Stir-Fry

Preparation Time: 30 minutes | Yield: 4 Servings

Ingredients:

- 1 head cauliflower cut into florets
- 3/4 cup onion white, thinly sliced
- 5 cloves garlic finely sliced
- 1 1/2 tablespoons tamari or gluten free tamari
- 1 tablespoon rice vinegar
- 1/2 teaspoon coconut sugar
- 1 tablespoon Sriracha or other favorite hot sauce
- 2 scallions for garnish

Directions:

Place cauliflower in the air fryer. If your air fryer is one that has holes in the bottom you'll need to use an air fryer insert. Set the temp to 350 degrees. Cook 10 minutes. Open the air fryer, grab the pot by the handle, remove and shake and slide back in the compartment. Add the sliced onion, stir and cook 10 more minutes. Add garlic, stir and cook 5 more minutes. Mix soy sauce, rice vinegar, coconut sugar, Sriracha, salt & pepper together in a small bowl.Add the mixture to cauliflower and stir. Cook 5 more minutes. The insert keeps all of the juices inside. To serve sprinkle sliced scallions over the top for garnish.

Nutritional Information:

Calories: 93, Fat: 3g, Carbs: 12g, Protein: 4g

Air Fried Cauliflower Rice

Preparation Time: 20 minutes | Yield: 3 Servings

Ingredients:

Round 1

- 1/2 block firm or extra firm tofu
- 2 tablespoons reduced sodium soy sauce
- 1/2 cup diced onion
- 1 cup diced carrot - about 1 1/2 to 2 carrots
- 1 teaspoon turmeric

Round 2

- 3 cups riced cauliflower - Cauliflower minced into pieces smaller than the size of a pea. You can do this by hand with a box-style cheese crater, use your food processor to pulse into pieces, or buy pre-riced, bagged cauliflower.
- 2 tablespoons reduced sodium soy sauce
- 1 1/2 teaspoons toasted sesame oil - optional, but recommended
- 1 tablespoon rice vinegar
- 1 tablespoon minced ginger
- 1/2 cup finely chopped broccoli
- 2 cloves garlic – minced
- 1/2 cup frozen peas

Directions:

In a large bowl, crumble the tofu (you're going for scrambled egg-size pieces, not ricotta here), then toss with the rest of the Round 1 ingredients. Air fry at 370F for 10 minutes, shaking once. Meanwhile, toss together all of the Round 2 ingredients in a large bowl. When that first 10 minutes of cooking are done, add all of the Round 2 ingredients to your air fryer, shake gently, and fry at 370 for 10 more minutes, shaking after 5 minutes. Riced cauliflower can vary quite a bit in size, so if you feel like yours doesn't look done enough at this point, you can cook for an additional 2-5 minutes at 370F. Just shake and check in every couple of minutes until it's done to your liking.

Nutritional Information:

Calories: 153, Fat: 3g, Carbs: 12g, Protein: 10g

Air Fried Sticky Mushroom Rice

Preparation Time: 20 minutes | Yield: 6 Servings

Ingredients:

- 16 ounces jasmine rice uncooked
- 1/2 cup soy sauce you can use gluten free tamari
- 4 tablespoons maple syrup
- 4 cloves garlic finely chopped
- 2 teaspoon Chinese 5 Spice
- 1/2 teaspoon ground ginger
- 4 tablespoons white wine you can use rice vinegar
- 16 ounces cremini mushrooms wiped clean, you can cut any huge mushrooms in half
- 1/2 cup peas frozen

Directions:

Start your rice now so that it will be done and hot at the same time as the sauce. Mix the next 6 ingredients together and set aside. Place the mushrooms in the air fryer. If you can set your degrees - set it to 350 degrees. Otherwise just turn it on. My Air Fryer temp is built in and always cooks at 338 degrees. Cook for 10 minutes. Open the air fryer, if you don't have one that stirs itself, pull out the pot and shake. Pour the liquid mixture and peas over the top of the mushrooms. Stir and cook 5 more minutes. Pour the mushroom/pea sauce over the pot of rice and stir. Serve.

Nutritional Information:

Calories: 366, Fat: 1g, Carbs: 77g, Protein: 10g

Air-Fried Asparagus

Preparation Time: 20 minutes | Yield: 2 Servings

Ingredients:

- 1/2 bunch of asparagus, with bottom 2 inches trimmed off
- Avocado or Olive Oil in an oil mister or sprayer
- 1 tsp. Himalayan salt
- 1/ tsp Black pepper

Directions:

Place trimmed asparagus spears in the air-fryer basket. Spritz spears lightly with oil, then sprinkle with salt and a tiny bit of black pepper. Place basket inside air-fryer and bake at 400° for 10 minutes. Serve immediately.

Nutritional Information:

Calories: 118, Fat: 8g, Carbs: 10g, Protein: 5g

Air Fried Zucchini, Yellow Squash, and Carrots

Preparation Time: 20 minutes | Yield: 2 Servings

Ingredients:

- ½ pound carrots, peeled and cut into 1-inch cubes
- 6 teaspoons olive oil
- 1 pound zucchini, stem and root ends trimmed and cut into ¾-inch half moons
- 1 pound yellow squash, stem and root ends trimmed and cut into ¾-inch half moons
- 1 teaspoon kosher salt
- ½ teaspoon ground white pepper
- 1 tablespoon tarragon leaves, roughly chopped

Directions:

In a small bowl, combine the carrot cubes with 2 teaspoons of the olive oil and toss well to combine. Place the carrots in the basket of the Air Fryer and close the drawer. Set the temperature to 400 degrees Fahrenheit and the timer to 5 minutes. While the carrots cook, place the zucchini and yellow squash pieces in a medium bowl. Drizzle with the remaining 4 teaspoons of olive oil and season with the salt and pepper. Toss well to coat the vegetables evenly. Once the timer goes off, add the zucchini and yellow squash to the basket of the Air Fryer along with the carrots and close the drawer. Set the timer for 30 minutes and cook the vegetables, tossing two or three times throughout the cooking process to ensure even browning. When the timer goes off, remove the vegetables from the Air Fryer and toss with the tarragon. Serve warm.

Nutritional Information:

Calories: 118, Fat: 8g, Carbs: 10g, Protein: 5g

Healthy Mediterranean Vegetables

Preparation Time: 20 minutes | Yield: Servings

Ingredients:

- 50 g Cherry Tomatoes
- 1 Large Courgette
- 1 Green Pepper
- 1 Large Parsnip
- 1 Medium Carrot
- 1 Tsp Mixed Herbs

- 2 Tbsp Honey
- 1 Tsp Mustard
- 2 Tsp Garlic Puree
- 6 Tbsp Olive Oil
- Salt & Pepper

Directions:

In the bottom of your Airfryer (chopping as you go) slice up the courgette and green pepper. Peel and dice the parsnip and carrot and add the cherry tomatoes whole while still on the vine for extra flavour. Drizzle with three tablespoons of olive oil and cook for 15 minutes at 180c. In the meantime mix up the rest of your ingredients into an Air fryer safe baking dish. When the vegetables are done transfer them from the bottom of the Airfryer into the baking dish and shake well so that all the vegetables are covered in the marinade. Sprinkle with a little more salt and pepper and cook for 5 minutes on 200c. Serve.

Nutritional Information:

Calories: 280, Fat: 21g, Carbs: 21g, Protein: 2g

Lemony Green Beans

Preparation Time: 10 minutes | Yield: 2 Servings

Ingredients:

- 1 lb. green beans, washed and destemmed
- 1 lemon
- Pinch of salt
- Black pepper to taste
- 1/4 teaspoon oil

Directions:

Put green beans in air fryer. Add a few squeezes of lemon. Add salt and pepper. Drizzle oil over top. Cook in Air Fryer at 400 degrees for 10-12 minutes.

Nutritional Information:

Calories: 52, Fat: 3g, Carbs: 5g, Protein: 1g

Crispy Roasted Broccoli

Preparation Time: 10 minutes | Yield: 2 Servings

Ingredients:

- 2 tbsps yogurt
- 1 tbsp chickpea flour
- 1/4 tsp turmeric powder
- 1/2 tsp salt
- 1/2 tsp red chilli powder
- 1/4 tsp masala chat

Directions:

To prepare crispy roasted broccoli, we need to cut the broccoli into small florets. Soak in a bowl of water with 2 tsp salt for 30 minutes to remove any impurities or worms. Remove the broccoli florets from the water. Drain well and wipe thoroughly using a kitchen towel to absorb all the moisture. In a bowl, mix together all the ingredients for the marinade. Toss the broccoli florets in this marinade. Cover and keep aside in the refrigerator for 15 minutes. When the broccoli is marinated, preheat the airfryer at 200°C. Open the basket of the airfryer and place the marinated florets inside. Push the basket back in, and turn the time dial to 10 minutes. Give the basket a shake once midway and then check after 10 minutes if golden and crisp. If not, keep for another 2-3 minutes. Eat them hot! If you don't have an air fryer, use a preheated oven and spread the florets on a lined baking tray and bake for around 15 minutes in a preheated oven at 190°C or until golden and crisp.

Nutritional Information:

Calories: 96, Fat: 1g, Carbs: 15g, Protein: 7g

Roasted Rainbow Vegetables

Preparation Time: 20 minutes | Yield: 4 Servings

Ingredients:

- 1 red bell pepper, seeded and cut into 1-inch pieces
- 1 yellow summer squash, cut into 1-inch pieces
- 1 zucchini, cut into 1-inch pieces
- 4 ounces fresh mushrooms, cleaned and halved
- 1/2 sweet onion, cut into 1-inch wedges
- 1 tablespoon extra-virgin olive oil
- salt and pepper to taste

Directions:

Preheat an air fryer according to manufacturer's recommendations. Place red bell pepper, summer squash, zucchini, mushrooms, and onion in a large bow. Add olive oil, salt, and black pepper and toss to combine. Place vegetables in an even layer in the air fryer basket. Air-fry vegetables until roasted, about 20 minutes, stirring halfway through cooking time.

Nutritional Information:

Calories: 69, Fat: 4g, Carbs: 7g, Protein: 3g

Keto Vegetable Recipes

Three Cheese Stuffed Mushrooms

Preparation Time: 15 minutes | Yield: 6 Servings

Ingredients:

- 8 oz large fresh mushrooms (I used Monterrery)
- 4 oz cream cheese (I used reduced-fat)
- ¼ cup parmesan cheese shredded
- salt and pepper to taste

- 1/8 cup sharp cheddar cheese shredded
- 1/8 cup white cheddar cheese shredded
- 1 teaspoon Worcesteshire sauce
- 2 garlic cloves chopped

Directions:

Cut the stem out of the mushroom to prepare it for stuffing. I first chop off the stem, and then make a circular cut around the area where the stem was. Continue to cut until you have removed excess mushroom. Place the cream cheese in the microwave for 15 seconds to soften. Combine the cream cheese, all of the shredded cheeses, salt, pepper, and Worcesteshire sauce in a medium bowl. Stir to combine. Stuff the mushrooms with the cheese mixture. Place the mushrooms in the Air Fryer for 8 minutes on 370 degrees. Allow the mushrooms to cool before serving.

Nutritional Information:

Calories: 116, Fat: 8g, Carbs: 3g, Protein: 8g

Air Fryer roasted Asian broccoli

Preparation Time: 20 minutes | Yield: 4 Servings

Ingredients:

- 1 Lb Broccoli, Cut into florets
- 1 1/2 Tbsp Peanut oil
- 1 Tbsp Garlic, minced
- Salt
- 2 Tbsp Reduced sodium soy sauce
- 2 tsp Stevia
- 2 tsp Sriracha
- 1 tsp Rice vinegar
- 1/3 Cup Roasted salted peanuts
- Fresh lime juice (optional)

Directions:

In a large bowl, toss together the broccoli, peanut oil, garlic and season with sea salt. Make sure the oil covers all the broccoli florets. I like to use my hands to give each one a quick rub. Spread the broccoli into the wire basket of your air fryer, in as single of a layer, as possible, trying to leave a little bit of space between each floret. Cook at 400 degrees until golden brown and crispy, about 15 – 20 minutes, stirring halfway. While the broccoli and peanuts cook, mix together the stevia, soy sauce, sriracha and rice vinegar in a small, microwave-safe bowl. Once mixed, microwave the mixture for 10-15 seconds. Transfer the cooked broccoli to a bowl and add in the soy sauce mixture. Toss to coat and season to taste with a pinch more salt, if needed. Stir in the peanuts and squeeze lime on top (if desired.) Devour!

Nutritional Information:

Calories: 68, Fat: 4g, Carbs: 2G, Protein: 1G

Cauliflower Buffalo Wings

Preparation Time: 15 minutes | Yield: 4 Servings

Ingredients:

- 1 head cauliflower cut into small bites
- cooking oil spray
- 1 tablespoon butter melted
- salt and pepper to taste
- 1/2 cup buffalo sauce

Directions:

Spray the air fryer basket with cooking oil. Add the melted butter, buffalo sauce, and salt and pepper to taste to a bowl. Stir to combine. Add the cauliflower bites to the air fryer. Spray with cooking oil. Cook for 7 minutes on 400 degrees. Open the air fryer and place the cauliflower in a large mixing bowl. Drizzle the butter and buffalo mixture throughout. Stir. Add the cauliflower back to the air fryer. Cook for an additional 7-8 minutes on 400 degrees until the cauliflower wings are crisp. Every air fryer brand is different. Be sure to use your personal judgment to assist with optimal cook time. Remove the cauliflower from the air fryer.

Nutritional Information:

Calories: 101, Fat: 7g, Carbs: 4g, Protein: 3g

Air Fryer Herbed Brussels Sprouts

Preparation Time: 10 minutes │ Yield: 4 Servings

Ingredients:

- 1 lb. brussels sprouts (cleaned and trimmed)
- 1/2 tsp. dried thyme
- 1 tsp. dried parsley
- 1 tsp. garlic powder (Or 4 cloves, minced)
- 1/4 tsp. salt
- 2 tsp. oil

Directions:

Place all ingredients in a medium to large mixing bowl and toss to coat the brussels sprouts evenly. Pour them into the food basket of the air fryer and close it up. Set the heat to 390 F. and the time to 8 minutes. This setting roasts them nicely on the outside while leaving the insides a nicely cooked al dente. Cool slightly and serve.

Nutritional Information:

Calories: 79, Fat: 2G, Carbs: 12G, Protein: 4g

Cilantro Ranch Sweet Potato Cauliflower Patties

Preparation Time: 20 minutes │ Yield: 7 Servings

Ingredients:

- 1 medium to large sweet potato, peeled
- 2 cup cauliflower florets
- 1 green onion, chopped.
- 1 tsp minced garlic
- 2 tbsp organic ranch seasoning mix or paleo ranch seasoning (dairy free)
- 1 cup packed cilantro (fresh)
- 1/2 tsp chili powder
- 1/4 tsp cumin
- 2 tbsp arrowroot starch or gluten free flour of choice
- 1/4 cup ground flaxseed
- 1/4 cup sunflower seeds (or pumpkin seeds)
- 1/4 tsp Kosher Salt and pepper (or to taste)
- Dipping sauce of choice

Directions

Cut your peeled sweet potato into smaller pieces. Place in a food processor or blender and pulse until the larger pieces are broken up. Add in your cauliflower, onion, and garlic and pulse again. Add in you sunflower seeds, flaxseed, arrowroot (or flour), cilantro, and remaining seasonings. Pulse or place on medium until a thick batter is formed. See blog for picture. Place batter in larger bowl. Scoop 1/4 cup of the batter out at a time and form into patties about 1.5 inches thick. Place on baking sheet. Repeat until you have about 7-10 patties. Chill in freeze for 10 minutes so the patties can set. Once set, Place cauliflower patties (4 at a time) in air fryer at 360 to 370F for 18 minutes, flipping halfway. If your patties are extra thick, they could take closer to 20 minutes.

Nutritional Information:

Calories: 85, Fat: 3g, Carbs: 9g, Protein: 3g

Air-Fried Asparagus

Preparation Time: 15 minutes | Yield: 2 Servings

Ingredients:

- 1/2 bunch of asparagus, with bottom 2 inches trimmed off
- Black pepper
- Avocado or Olive Oil in an oil mister or sprayer
- Himalayan salt

Directions:

Place trimmed asparagus spears in the air-fryer basket. Spritz spears lightly with oil, then sprinkle with salt and a tiny bit of black pepper. Place basket inside air-fryer and bake at 400° for 10 minutes. Serve immediately.

Nutritional Information:

Calories: 45, Fat: 3g, Carbs: 3g, Protein: 2G

Cauliflower Tater Tots

Preparation Time: 15 minutes | Yield: 4 Servings

Ingredients:

- 1 large head of cauliflower separated into large florets
- 2 large Eggs
- 1/4 cup Coconut Flour
- 1 tsp Garlic Powder

- 1 tsp Onion Powder
- Coconut Oil spray or mist
- 1 tsp dried Parsley
- Salt and Pepper to taste

Directions:

Separate the cauliflower into large florets. In a large microwaveable bowl, add the florets and 2 tablespoons of water. Cover with a plastic wrap and microwave for 3 to 5 minutes (depending on the power of your microwave). The floret should be tender but not mushy. Initially microwave for 3 minutes. If underdone, microwave for another minute or two. Drain well. Combine the florets in a chopper or food processor and process, till it resembles grains of rice. Pour it in a bowl. Add the beaten eggs, coconut flour, garlic powder, onion powder, dried parsley, salt and pepper. Mix well. Take a small amount of the mix and shape it like tater tots. Chill the cauliflower tots for 30 minutes. Liberally grease the air fryer basket. Place the cauliflower tots in a single layer and spray with coconut oil or mist. Air fry at 400 F for 12 minutes. Serve hot with Paleo Ketchup or condiment of choice.

Nutritional Information:

Calories: 142, Fat: 11G, Carbs: 3g

Air Fryer Pumpkin French Fries

Preparation Time: 15 minutes Yield: 4 Servings

Ingredients:

- 250g Pumpkin
- 1 Tsp Thyme
- 1 Tbsp Mustard
- Salt & Pepper
- Tomato Ketchup optional

Directions:

Peel the pumpkin remove the seeds and slice into French Fries. Place them in the Airfryer at 390 degrees for 15 minutes. Half way through, shake and season with the thyme, mustard, salt and pepper. Serve hot with tomato ketchup.

Nutritional Information:

Calories: 142, Fat: 10G, Carbs: 6g, Protein: 3g

Air Fryer Keto Falafel

Preparation Time: 15 minutes Yield: 4 Servings

Ingredients:

- 1 cup (170G) brined lupini beans
- 1 1/2 cups (150G) thawed frozen broccoli
- 1/4 cup (60g) tahini
- 2 tbsp lemon juice
- 1 tbsp dried parsley
- 2 tsp cumin
- 2 tbsp ground chia seeds
- 1/2 tsp garlic powder
- 1/4 tsp onion powder
- 1/4 tsp all spice

Directions:

Before you start, soak the lupini beans in hot water for between 30-60 minutes and then drain them. This should help to temper some of the overly briney flavor. In a food processor, chop the beans and broccoli until they are in pieces, about the size of a grain of rice (you can even go smaller, if you have the patience!). Transfer this mixture to a medium sized mixing bowl. Add the tahini, lemon juice and seasoning to the mixture and stir until thoroughly combined. Stir in the ground chia seeds completely and let the mixture sit for about 5 minutes, so the chia can absorb some liquid and a thick dough forms. Shape the dough mixture into 12 patties - I started with a golfball-sized ball of dough, and then flattened them to be about 5cm (2 inches) across and 1CM (a little less than 1/2 inch) thick. Arrange the patties in your air fryer in a single layer, and cook at 350F(177C) for 14-15 minutes, depending on how crunchy you like them! Enjoy while warm. To reheat these, I stuck them back in the air fryer for around 8 minutes at the same temp.

Nutritional Information:

Calories: 188, Fat: 12G, Carbs: 5g, Protein: 11g

Keto Air Fryer Roasted Cauliflower with Tahini Sauce

Preparation Time: 25 minutes | Yield: 4 Servings

Ingredients:

- 5 cups chopped cauliflower about 1 large head of cauliflower
- 6 cloves garlic peeled and chopped

- 4 tablespoons vegetable oil
- 1 teaspoon cumin coriander blend
- 1/2 tsp salt

For the Sauce

- 2 tablespoons tahini sesame paste
- 2 tablespoons hot water
- 1 tablespoons fresh lemon juice

- 1 teaspoon minced garlic
- 1/2 teaspoon salt

Directions:

Chop the cauliflower into evenly-sized florets and put them in a large bowl. Cut each garlic clove into 3 pieces and smash them down with the side of your knife. Don't be shy about smashing the garlic. You want to expose as much of the garlicky surface area as possible so that it roasts well. Add this to the cauliflower. Pour over the oil and add salt and the cumin coriander blend. Mix well until the cauliflower is well-coated with the oil and the spices. Turn your airfryer to 400F for 20 minutes and add the cauliflower, flipping once at the halfway mark.

Make The Sauce:

While the cauliflower cooks, make the sauce. In a small bowl, add the Tahini, hot water, lemon juice, minced garlic, and salt. As soon as you do this, you will see a curdled murky mess and you'll wonder if you messed up. You haven't messed up. Just stir and keep stirring until you get a thick, creamy, smooth mix with the tahini and water. One the cauliflower is cooked, place it into a large serving bowl. Pour the tahini sauce over the cauliflower and mix well, and then serve.

Nutritional Information:

Calories: 207, Fat: 18G, Carbs: 10G, Protein: 4g

Dessert Recipes

Nutella-Banana Sandwiches

Preparation Time: 10 minutes | Yield: 2 Servings

Ingredients:

- ½ cup butter, softened
- 4 slices white bread

- ¼ cup chocolate hazelnut spread (Nutella)
- 1 banana

Directions:

Pre-heat the air fryer to 370°F. Spread the softened butter on one side of all the slices of bread and place the slices, buttered side down on the counter. Spread the chocolate hazelnut spread on the other side of the bread slices. Cut the banana in half and then slice each half into three slices lengthwise. Place the banana slices on two slices of bread and top with the remaining slices of bread to make two sandwiches. Cut the sandwiches in half (triangles or rectangles) – this will help them all fit in the air fryer at once. Transfer the sandwiches to the air fryer. Air-fry at 370°F for 5 minutes. Flip the sandwiches over and air-fry for another 2 to 3 minutes, or until the top bread slices are nicely browned. Pour yourself a glass of milk or a midnight nightcap while the sandwiches cool slightly and enjoy!!

Nutritional Information:

Calories: 237, Fat: 14g, Carbs: 26g, Protein: 3g

Molten Lava Cake

Preparation Time: 10 minutes | Yield: 4 Servings

Ingredients:

- 1.5 TBS Self Rising Flour
- 2 Eggs
- 3.5 TBS Baker's Sugar (Not Powdered)
- 3.5 OZ Unsalted Butter
- 3.5 OZ Dark Chocolate (Pieces or Chopped)

Directions:

Preheat your Air Fryer to 375F. Grease and flour 4 standard oven safe ramekins. Melt dark chocolate and butter in a microwave safe bowl on level 7 for 3 minutes, stirring throughout. Remove from microwave and stir until even consistency. Whisk/Beat the eggs and sugar until pale and frothy. Pour melted chocolate mixture into egg mixture. Stir in flour. Use a spatula to combine everything evenly. Fill the ramekins about 3/4 full with cake mixture and bake in preheated air fryer at 375F for 10 minutes. Remove from the air fryer and allow to cool in ramekin for 2 minutes. Carefully turn ramekins upside down onto serving plate, tapping the bottom with a butter knife to loosen edges. Cake should release from the ramekin with a little effort and center should appear dark/gooey. Enjoy warm a-la-mode or with a raspberry drizzle.

Nutritional Information:

Calories: 540, Fat: 14g, Carbs: 53g, Protein: 4g

Shortbread Heart Cookies

Preparation Time: 10 minutes | Yield: 2 Servings

Ingredients:

- 250 g Plain Flour
- 75 g Caster Sugar
- 175 g Butter
- 1 Tsp Vanilla Essence
- Chocolate Buttons

Directions:

Preheat the air fryer to 180c. In a mixing bowl place all your ingredients apart from your chocolate and rub the fat into the other ingredients. It will soon rub into each other to create a nice soft dough.When it is a big dough ball roll it out and cut it into heart shapes with your cutter. Place it into the air fryer on top of a baking sheet with a little gap in between each one. Cook for 10 minutes on 180c. Open the air fryer and place the chocolate buttons into the top of the half baked dough. Cook for a further 10 minutes on 160c and serve with hot chocolate and marshmallows.

Nutritional Information:

Calories: 190, Fat: 11g, Carbs: 21g, Protein: 2g

Vegan Beignets

Preparation Time: 20 minutes | Yield: 4 Servings

Ingredients:

FOR THE POWDERED BAKING BLEND:

- 1 cup Whole Earth Sweetener Baking Blend
- 1 teaspoon organic corn starch

FOR THE PROOFING:

- 1 cup full-fat coconut milk from a can
- 3 tablespoons powdered baking blend
- 1 1/2 teaspoons active baking yeast

FOR THE DOUGH:

- 2 tablespoons melted coconut oil
- 2 tablespoons drained water from a can of chickpeas
- 2 teaspoons vanilla
- 3 cups unbleached white flour, with a little extra to sprinkle on the cutting board for later

Directions:

Add the Whole Earth Baking Blend and corn starch to your blender and blend until powdery smooth. The cornstarch will keep it from clumping so you can store it if you don't use it all in the recipe. Heat the coconut milk until it's warm but cool enough that you can stick your finger in it without burning yourself. If it's too hot, you will kill the yeast. Add it to your mixer with the sugar and yeast. Let sit 10 minutes, until the yeast begins to foam. Using the paddle attachment, mix in the coconut oil, aquafaba, and vanilla. Then add the flour a cup at a time. Once the flour is mixed in and the dough is coming away from the sides of the mixer, change to your dough hook if you have one. (If you don't, keep using the paddle.) Knead the dough in your mixer for about 3 minutes. The dough will be wetter than if you were making a loaf of bread, but you should be able to scrape out the dough and form a ball without it staying on your hands. Place dough in a mixing bowl and cover with a clean dish towel and let rise for 1 hour. Sprinkle some flour over a large cutting board and pat out the dough into a rectangle that's about ⅓ inch thick. Cut into 24 squares and let it proof for 30 minutes before you cook them. Preheat your air fryer to 390 degrees. Depending on the size of your air fryer you can put 3 to 6 beignets in at a time. Cook for 3 minutes on one side. Flip them, then cook another 2 minutes. Since air fryers vary, you may need to cook yours another minute or two for them to get golden brown. Sprinkle liberally with the powdered baking blend you made in the beginning and enjoy! Continue cooking in batches until they are all cooked. Preheat your oven to 350 degrees. Place the beignets on a baking sheet covered with parchment paper. Bake for about 15 minutes or until golden brown. Sprinkle liberally with the powdered baking blend you made in the beginning and enjoy!

Nutritional Information:

Calories: 102, Fat: 3g, Carbs: 15g, Protein: 3g

Apple Pie

Preparation Time: 30 minutes | Yield: 4 Servings

Ingredients:

- 1 Pillsbury Refrigerator pie crust
- Baking spray
- 1 large apple, chopped
- 2 teaspoons lemon juice
- 1 tablespoon ground cinnamon

- 2 tablespoon sugar
- ½ teaspoon vanilla extract
- 1 tablespoon butter
- 1 beaten egg
- 1 tablespoon raw sugar

Directions:

Defrost pre made pie crust according to package directions. Pre-heat the Airfryer on the highest degree while you are preparing the pie. Using the smaller baking tin, cut 1 crust about an ⅛ of an inch larger than the tin and a second one a little smaller than the baking tin. You may need to roll the crust a tiny bit with a rolling pin to stretch the pie crust. Set the smaller one aside. Spray the baking tin with the baking spray and place the larger cut crust into the baking pan. Set aside. In a small bowl, place the chopped apple, lemon juice, cinnamon, sugar, and vanilla extract. Mix to combine. Pour the apples into the baking pan with the pie crust. Top apples with pieces of butter. Place the second pie crust over the top of the apples and pinch edge. Make a few slits in the top of the dough. Spread beaten egg over the top of the crust and sprinkle raw sugar over the top of the egg mixture. Place pie in Air Fryer basket. Set the timer for 30 minutes at 320 Degrees

Nutritional Information:

Calories: 243, Fat: 10g, Carbs: 36g, Protein: 5g

Zebra Butter Cake

Preparation Time: 30 minutes | Yield: 4 Servings

Ingredients:

- 115g butter
- 2 eggs
- 100g castor sugar
- 100g self raising flour, sifted
- 30ml milk
- 1tsp vanilla extract
- 1 tbsp of cocoa powder

Directions:

Preheat airfryer at 160C. Line the 6" baking tin base and grease the side of the tin. Beat butter and sugar in mixer till fluffy. Add eggs one at a time then add vanilla extract and milk. Mix well in mixer. Add sifted flour and mix till incorporated. Scoop half batter out and set aside. Add cocoa powder to the batter in mixer and mix well. Scoop 2 tablespoons of the plain batter on center of baking tin. Then scoop 2 tablespoons of chocolate batter on the centre of the plain batter in the baking tin. Keep scooping by alternating both batters until finish. After every scoop of batter into the tin, try to tap the tin to let batter spread out. Place baking tin in airfryer and bake at 160C for 30 minutes or until the skewer emerges cleanly.

Nutritional Information:

Calories: 380, Fat: 17g, Carbs: 55g, Protein: 2g

Thai-Style Fried Bananas

Preparation Time: 40 minutes | Yield: 4 Servings

Ingredients:

- 4 Ripe Bananas
- 2 tablespoons All Purpose Flour
- 2 tablespoons Rice flour
- 2 tablespoons Corn flour
- 2 tablespoons Desiccated Coconut
- 1 pinch Salt
- 1/2 teaspoon Baking powder
- 1/2 teaspoon Cardamom Powder, (optional)
- Cooking oil, to drizzle
- 1/4 cup Rice flour, for coating
- Sesame seeds, for coating

Directions:

To begin making the Fried Bananas, get all the ingredients together and keep them handy. We will begin by making the batter for the fried bananas. Into a large bowl, add in the all purpose flour, rice flour, corn flour, baking powder, salt, coconut and stir to combine well. Next add in little water at a time to make a thick and almost smooth batter. The batter should be such that it can coat the back of a spoon. Keep the rice flour and sesame seeds ready. If you are using mini bananas (almost a large finger size), then slice it lengthwise into half. If you are using a large banana, then cut it into half, then slice it half lengthwise. Keep it aside. Next grease a 8 x 8 inch foil or a butter paper with oil and dust it with flour. This is so that when we air fry the batter dipped bananas, they don't stick to the foil or the paper. Fit the foil or the butter paper pinching the ends so as to leave a little gap for air circulation. Dip banana slices into the wet batter, then roll the wet batter coated banana slices into the dry rice flour and then onto the sesame seeds. I like adding sesame seeds to the top as it adds a crunchiness to the air fried bananas. Place the batter dipped bananas into the greased foil or butter paper. Air fry the bananas at 200C for about 10 to 15 minutes, flipping half way through so it gets fried evenly all around. Once ready, serve the Thai Crispy Fried Bananas as a tea time snack or even as a dessert served along with vanilla ice cream.

Nutritional Information:

Calories: 378, Fat: 22g, Carbs: 44g, Protein: 5g

Air Fryer Cinnamon Rolls

Preparation Time: 20 minutes | Yield: 8 Servings

Ingredients:

- 1 pound frozen bread dough, thawed
- ¼ cup butter, melted and cooled
- ¾ cup brown sugar
- 1½ tablespoons ground cinnamon

Cream Cheese Glaze:

- 4 ounces cream cheese, softened
- 2 tablespoons butter, softened
- 1¼ cups powdered sugar
- ½ teaspoon vanilla

Directions:

Let the bread dough come to room temperature on the counter. On a lightly floured surface roll the dough into a 13-inch by 11-inch rectangle. Position the rectangle so the 13-inch side is facing you. Brush the melted butter all over the dough, leaving a 1-inch border uncovered along the edge farthest away from you. Combine the brown sugar and cinnamon in a small bowl. Sprinkle the mixture evenly over the buttered dough, keeping the 1-inch border uncovered. Roll the dough into a log starting with the edge closest to you. Roll the dough tightly, making sure to roll evenly and push out any air pockets. When you get to the uncovered edge of the dough, press the dough onto the roll to seal it together. Cut the log into 8 pieces, slicing slowly with a sawing motion so you don't flatten the dough. Turn the slices on their sides and cover with a clean kitchen towel. Let the rolls sit in the warmest part of your kitchen for 1½ to 2 hours to rise. To make the glaze, place the cream cheese and butter in a microwave-safe bowl. Soften the mixture in the microwave for 30 seconds at a time until it is easy to stir. Gradually add the powdered sugar and stir to combine. Add the vanilla extract and whisk until smooth. Set aside. When the rolls have risen, pre-heat the air fryer to 350°F. Transfer 4 of the rolls to the air fryer basket. Air-fry for 5 minutes. Turn the rolls over and air-fry for another 4 minutes. Repeat with the remaining 4 rolls. Let the rolls cool for a couple of minutes before glazing. Spread large dollops of cream cheese glaze on top of the warm cinnamon rolls, allowing some of the glaze to drip down the side of the rolls. Serve warm and enjoy!

Nutritional Information:

Calories: 143, Fat: 8g, Carbs: 17g, Protein: 1g

Air Fryer Cranberry Pecan Muffins

Preparation Time: 20 minutes | Yield: 8 Servings

Ingredients:

- 1/4 cup cashew milk (or use any dairy or non-dairy milk you prefer)
- 2 large eggs
- 1/2 tsp. vanilla extract
- 1 1/2 cups Almond Flour
- 1/4 cup Monkfruit (or use your preferred sweetener)
- 1/4 tsp. cinnamon
- 1/8 tsp. salt
- 1/2 cup fresh cranberries
- 1/4 cup chopped pecans
- 1 tsp. baking powder

Directions:

Add to blender jar the milk, eggs and vanilla extract and blend 20-30 seconds. Add in the almond flour, sugar, baking powder, cinnamon and salt – blend another 30-45 seconds until well blended. Removed the blender jar from the base and stir in the 1/2 of the fresh cranberries and the pecans. Add the mixture to silicone muffin cups. Top each of the muffins with remainder of fresh cranberries. Place the muffins into the air fryer basket and bake on 325 for 12-15 minutes – or until toothpick comes out clean. Remove from air fryer and cool on wire rack. Drizzle with a maple glaze if desired. I also drizzled melted white chocolate over some of the muffins.

Nutritional Information:

Calories: 143, Fat: 8g, Carbs: 17g, Protein: 1g

Air Fryer Homemade Pop Tarts

Preparation Time: 20 minutes | Yield: 6 Servings

Ingredients:

- 2 refrigerated pie crusts
- 1 tsp cornstarch
- 1/3 cup low-sugar strawberry preserve
- 1/2 cup plain, non-fat vanilla Greek yogurt
- 1 oz reduced-fat Philadelphia cream cheese
- 1 tsp sugar sprinkles
- 1 tsp stevia
- olive oil or coconut oil spray

Directions:

Lay the pie crust on a flat working surface. I used a bamboo cutting board. Using a knife or pizza cutter, cut the 2 pie crusts into 6 rectangles (3 from each pie crust). Each should be fairly long in length as you will fold it over to close the pop tart. Add the preserve and cornstarch to a bowl and mix well. Add a tablespoon of the preserve to the crust. Place the preserve in the upper area of the crust. Fold each over to close the pop tarts. Using a fork, make imprints in each of the pop tarts, to create vertical and horizontal lines along the edges. Place the pop tarts in the Air Fryer. Spray with oil. I prefer to use olive oil. Cook on 375 degrees for 10 minutes. You may want to check on the Pop Tarts around 8 minutes to ensure they aren't too crisp for your liking. Combine the Greek yogurt, cream cheese, and stevia in a bowl to create the frosting. Allow the Pop Tarts to cool before removing them from the Air Fryer. This is important. If you do not allow them to cool, they may break. Remove the pop tarts from the Air Fryer. Top each with the frosting. Sprinkle sugar sprinkles throughout.

Nutritional Information:

Calories: 274, Fat: 14g, Carbs: 32g, Protein: 3g

Keto Dessert Recipes

Chocolate Lava Cake

Preparation Time: 10 minutes | Yield: 4 Servings

Ingredients:

- 1 egg
- 2 tablespoons cocoa powder
- 2 tablespoons water
- 2 tablespoons non-GMO erythritol
- 1/8 teaspoon Stevia

- 1 tablespoon golden flax meal
- 1 tablespoon coconut oil, melted
- 1/2 teaspoon aluminum-free baking powder
- dash of vanilla
- pinch of Himalayan salt

Directions:

Whisk all ingredients in a two-cup glass Pyrex dish or ramekin. Preheat air fryer at 350° for just a minute. Place glass dish with cake mix into air fryer and bake at 350° for 8-9 minutes. Carefully remove dish with an oven mitt. Let cool for a few minutes and then enjoy!

Nutritional Information:

Calories: 173, Fat: 13G, Carbs: 4g, Protein: 8g

Keto Chocolate Cake

Preparation Time: 20 minutes | Yield: 4 Servings

Ingredients:

- 3 Eggs
- 1/3 cup Truvia
- 4 tablespoons butter

- 2 tablespoon unsweetened Cocoa powder
- 1/4 TEASPOON SALT

- 1/2 cup heavy whipping cream
- 1 teaspoon Vanilla extract
- 1/4 cup Coconut Flour
- 1 teaspoon baking powder

Frosting
- 4 tablespoons Cream cheese softened
- 4 tablespoons Butter unsalted softened
- 1 tablespoon Truvia
- 1 teaspoon Vanilla extract

Directions:

Preheat the Breville Smart Oven Air or your regular oven to 350F degrees. Grease a silicone flower cupcake mold or a 6-cup muffin pan and set aside. In a large mixing bowl, melt the butter in the microwave for 30-60 seconds. Remove and stir in the Truvia into the butter. Add in eggs, heavy whipping cream, and vanilla extract and beat with a mixer. Stop the mixer and add in all the dry ingredients into the bowl. Mix again until the batter is well-mixed and relatively smooth. Coconut flours vary in absorbency. If the batter is thicker than regular cake batter, add in a little more heavy whipping cream and mix. Pour the batter into the silicone flower cupcake mold pan (or 6-cup muffin pan). Bake for 20 minutes until the tops spring back lightly when touched and a toothpick inserted emerges clean. Allow to cool
To make the Frosting: Beat together all four ingredients and spread on cooled cupcakes.

Nutritional Information:

Calories: 296, Fat: 28G, Carbs: 5g, Protein: 4g

Air Fried Sweet Potato Dessert Fries

Preparation Time: 25 minutes | Yield: 4 Servings

Ingredients:

- 2 medium sweet potatoes and/or yams peeled (see notes for low carb option)
- Half a tablespoon of coconut oil.
  - 1 tablespoon arrowroot starch or cornstarch
  - Optional 2 tsp melted butter (for coating)
  - 1/4 cup coconut sugar or raw sugar
- 1 to 2 tablespoons cinnamon
- Optional powdered sugar for dusting (see notes for sugar free option)

Dipping Sauces
- Dessert Hummus
- Honey or Vanilla Greek Yogurt
- Maple Frosting (vegan)

Directions:

Peel your sweet potatoes and wash them with clean water, then dry. Slice peeled sweet potatoes lengthwise, 1/2 inch thick. Toss your sweet potato slices in 1/2 tbsp coconut oil and arrowroot starch (or cornstarch). Place in air fryer for 18 minutes at 370F. Shake halfway at 8-9 minutes. Remove the fries from the air fryer and place in large bowl. Drizzle 2 tsp optional butter on top of fries. Then mix in cinnamon and sugar and toss fries together again. Place on plate to serve, sprinkle with powdered sugar. Serve fries with dipping sauce of choice. To store, keep fries wrapped in foil and in fridge. Then reheat in oven again to warm before serving. Should keep for 2-3 days.

For low sugar/carb options: Replace the sweet potato with peeled jicama sticks (baking times are similar). Use swerve sugar sweetener in place of powdered sugar and other sugars.

Nutritional Information:

Calories: 181, Fat: 11G, Carbs: 6g, Protein: 6g

Easy Coconut Pie

Preparation Time: 45 minutes | Yield: 6 Servings

Ingredients:

- 2 eggs
- 1 1/2 cups milk (you can use coconut milk or almond milk)
- 1/4 cup butter
- 1 1/2 tsp. vanilla extract
- 1 cup shredded coconut
- 1/2 cup Monk Fruit (or your preferred sugar)
- 1/2 cup coconut flour

Directions:

In a large bowl add in all the ingredients and using a wooden spoon stir until well blended. Coat a 6″ pie plate with non stick spray and fill it with the batter. Cook in the Air Fryer at 350 degrees for 10 to 12 minutes. Check the pie halfway thru the cooking time to be sure it is not burning, give the plate a turn, use a toothpick to test for doneness. Continue to cook accordingly. Toast ¼ cup of shredded coconut either in the oven or in a small fry pan for garnish (optional). Cool pie and garnish with shredded coconut and powdered sugar. Keep leftovers refrigerated.

Nutritional Information:

Calories: 281, Fat: 16G, Carbs: 18G, Protein: 3g

Air Fried Cheesecake Bites

Preparation Time: 10 minutes | Yield: 4 Servings

Ingredients:

- 8 ounces cream cheese
- 1/2 cup erythritol
- 2 Tablespoons cream, divided
- 1/2 teaspoon vanilla extract
- 1/2 cup almond flour
- 2 Tablespoons erythritol

Directions:

Allow the cream cheese to sit on the counter for 20 minutes to soften. Fit a stand mixer with paddle attachment. Mix the softened cream cheese, 1/2 cup erithrytol, vanilla and heavy cream until smooth. Scoop onto a parchment paper lined baking sheet. Freeze for about 30 minutes, until firm. Mix the almond flour with the 2 Tablespoons erythritol in a small mixing bowl. Dip the frozen cheesecake bites into 2 Tablespoons cream, then roll into the almond flour mixture. Place in an air fryer for 5 minutes.

Nutritional Information:

Calories: 90, Fat: 3g, Carbs: 16G, Protein: 1G

Chocolate Brownies

Preparation Time: 35 minutes | Yield: 4 Servings

Ingredients:

- 1/2 cup sugar-free chocolate chips
- 1/2 cup butter
- 3 eggs
- 1/4 cup Truvia or other sweetener
- 1 tsp Vanilla extract

Directions:

In a microwave safe bowl, melt butter and chocolate for about 1 minute. Remove and stir well. You really want to use the heat within the butter and chocolate to melt the rest of the clumps. If you microwave until it's all melted, you've overcooked the chocolate. So get a spoon and start stirring. Add 10 seconds if needed but stir well before you decide to do that. In a bowl, add eggs, sweetener, and vanilla and blend until light and frothy. Pour the melted butter and chocolate into the bowl in a slow stream and beat again until it is well-incorporated. Pour the mixture into greased springform container or cake pan and bake at 350F for 30-35 minutes until a knife inserted in the center emerges clean. Serve with whipped cream if desired

Nutritional Information:

Calories: 224, Fat: 23G, Carbs: 3g, Protein: 4g

Apple Cider Vinegar Donuts

Preparation Time: 10 minutes | Yield: 4 Servings

Ingredients:

For the Muffins

- 4 large eggs
- 4 tbsp coconut oil melted
- 3 tbsp Truvia or any other stevia you like
- 2/3 cup apple cider vinegar

- 1 cup coconut flour
- 1 tsp cinnamon
- 1 tsp baking soda
- pinch salt

Directions:

Preheat oven to 350 F. Prepare a donut baking pan by spraying liberally with cooking spray or greasing well with coconut oil. In a small bowl, whisk together the eggs, salt, stevia, apple cider vinegar and melted coconut oil. In a separate bowl, sift together cinnamon, baking soda and coconut flour to disperse the dry ingredients well. Add the dry ingredients to the wet ingredients until throughly combined. The batter will be a bit wet. Transfer the batter to the donut baking pan and scoop the batter into the cavities. Use your fingers to spread the batter evenly in the cavity. Bake at 350 F for 10 minutes until golden around the edges. Remove from the oven and cool in the baking 5-10 minutes before flipping onto a wire rack to remove. It's very important these are cool before you remove otherwise they will fall apart. They need to be a bit hard! Devour!

Nutritional Information:

Calories: 179, Fat: 11G, Carbs: 9g, Protein: 6g

Air-Fried Spiced Apples

Preparation Time: 15 minutes | Yield: 4 Servings

Ingredients:

- 4 small apples, sliced
- 2 tablespoons ghee or coconut oil, melted
- 1 cup granulated erythritol sweetener
- 1 teaspoon apple pie spice

Directions:

Place the apples in a bowl. Drizzle with ghee or coconut oil and sprinkle with erythritol and apple pie spice. Stir to evenly coat the apples. Place the apples in the air-fryer basket. Set the air fryer to 350° for 10 minutes. Pierce the apples with a fork to ensure they are tender. If needed place back in air fryer for an additional 3-5 minutes. Serve with ice cream or whipped topping.

Nutritional Information:

Calories: 112, Fat: 8g, Carbs: 2G, Protein: 3g

Air Fryer Brazilian Pineapple

Preparation Time: 25 minutes | Yield: 4 Servings

Ingredients:

- 1 small pineapple peeled, cored and cut into spears
- 1/2 cup brown sugar
- 2 teaspoons ground cinnamon
- 3 tablespoons melted butter

Directions:

In a small bowl, mix together brown sugar and cinnamon. Brush the pineapple spears with the melted butter. Sprinkle cinnamon sugar over the spears, pressing lightly to ensure it adheres well. Place the spears into the air fryer basket in a single layer. Depending on the size of your air fryer, you may have to do this in batches. Set fryer to 400°F for 10 minutes for the first batch (6-8 minutes for the next batch as your air fryer will be preheated). Halfway through, brush with any remaining butter. Pineapple spears are done when they are heated through and the sugar is bubbling.

Nutritional Information:

Calories: 295, Fat: 11G, Carbs: 40g

Coconut-Encrusted Cinnamon Bananas

Preparation Time: 25 minutes | Yield: 4 Servings

Ingredients:

- 4 ripe but firm Bananas cut into thirds
- 1/2 cup Tapioca Flour
- 2 large Eggs
- 1 cup Shredded Coconut Flakes
- 1 tsp Ground Cinnamon
- Coconut spray

Directions:

Cut each bananas into thirds. Make an assembly line . Pour the tapioca flour in to a shallow dish. Crack the eggs in another shallow bowl and whisk it lightly. Combine the shredded coconut and the ground cinnamon in the third shallow dish. Mix well. Dredge the bananas in tapioca flour and shake off the excess. Dip it in the beaten eggs. Make sure it is completely coated in egg wash. Roll the bananas in the cinnamon–coconut flakes to fully coat it. Press it firmly to make sure the coconut flakes are adhering to the bananas. Keep them in a flat tray. Liberally spray the air fryer basket with coconut oil. Arrange the coconut crusted bananas pieces in the fryer basket. Spray with more coconut spray. Air fry at 270F for 12 minutes. Dust with ground cinnamon and serve warm or at room temperature with a scoop of Low Carb ice-cream (optional).

Nutritional Information:

Calories: 155, Fat: 11G, Carbs: 20G, Protein: 2G

Asian Chicken Recipes

Flavorful Tandoori Chicken

Preparation Time: 10 minutes | Cooking Time: 15 minutes | Serve: 4

Ingredients:

- 1 lb chicken tenders, cut each in half
- 3/4 tsp garam masala
- ½ tsp turmeric
- ½ tsp chili powder
- ¼ cup fresh parsley, chopped
- 1 tbsp ginger garlic paste
- ¼ cup yogurt
- 1 tbsp olive oil
- ¾ tsp salt

Directions:

Add all ingredients except oil into the large bowl and mix well and set aside for 30 minutes. Preheat the air fryer to 350 F/ 180 C for 5 minutes. Spray air fryer basket from inside with cooking spray. Place marinated chicken into the air fryer basket. Brush chicken with olive oil. Air fry at 350 F/ 180 C for 10 minutes. Turn chicken to another side and air fry for 5 minutes more. Serve and enjoy.

Nutritional Value:

Calories 266, Fat 12.5 g, Carbohydrates 2.4 gs

Stir Fry Chicken

Preparation Time: 10 minutes | Cooking Time: 20 minutes | Serve: 4

Ingredients:

• 1 lb chicken breast, skinless, boneless, and cut into chunks • 1 ½ tsps white vinegar • 1 tsp sesame oil • 1 tbsp soy sauce • ½ tbsp ginger, minced	• ½ tsp garlic powder • 1 tbsp olive oil • 1 small onion, sliced • 1 cup broccoli florets • Pepper • Salt

Directions:

In a large mixing bowl, mix together chicken, onion, and broccoli. In a small bowl, mix together olive oil, vinegar, sesame oil, soy sauce, ginger, and garlic powder and pour over chicken and stir well. Transfer chicken mixture to air fryer basket and air fry at 380 F/195 C for 15-20 minutes. Shake air fryer basket halfway through. Make sure chicken is cooked. If not then air fry for 4-5 minutes more. Season with pepper and salt. Serve and enjoy.

Nutritional Value:

Calories 190, Fat 7.6 g, Carbohydrates 4.2 g

Spicy Chicken Wings

Preparation Time: 10 minutes | Cooking Time: 25 minutes | Serve: 4

Ingredients:

- 1 lb chicken wings
- ¼ cup cornstarch

- Pepper
- Salt

For sauce:

- ½ fresh lime juice
- 1 tbsp olive oil
- 1 ¼ tbsps soy sauce

- 1 ½ tbsps sriracha sauce
- 3 tbsp honey

Directions:

Preheat the air fryer to 375 F/ 190 C. In a large bowl, add chicken wings, cornstarch, pepper, and salt and toss until chicken wings are well coated. Spray air fryer basket from inside with cooking spray. Place chicken wings in the air fryer basket and air fry for 25 minutes. Turn chicken wings after every 5 minutes. Meanwhile, add all sauce ingredients into a small pan and bring to boil over low heat. Once wings are cooked then transfer them in mixing bowl. Pour sauce over chicken wings and toss well. Serve and enjoy.

Nutritional Value:

Calories 365, Fat 15.7 g, Carbohydrates 21.5 g

Delicious Chicken Thighs

Preparation Time: 10 minutes | Cooking Time: 25 minutes | Serve: 6

Ingredients:

- 6 chicken thighs, boneless
- ¾ tbsp onion powder
- ½ tbsp garlic powder
- 3 tbsps honey
- 2 tbsps lemon juice
- 1 tbsp Worcestershire sauce
- 3 tbsps soy sauce
- 1 tbsp sesame oil
- 2 tbsps olive oil
- ½ tsp kosher salt

Directions:

Add all ingredients into the large bowl and mix until chicken is well coated. Spray air fryer basket from inside with cooking spray. Place chicken into the air fryer basket and air fry at 400 F/ 200 C for 15 minutes. Turn chicken to other side and air fry for 10 minutes more. Serve and enjoy.

Nutritional Value:

Calories 383, Fat 17.8 g, Carbohydrates 11.1 g

Crispy Chicken Wings

Preparation Time: 10 minutes | Cooking Time: 34 minutes | Serve: 4

Ingredients:

- 2 lbs chicken wings
- ½ tsp onion powder
- 1 tsp garlic powder

- ½ cup cornstarch
- ½ tsp salt

For sauce:

- ½ tsp garlic, minced
- ½ tsp ginger, minced
- 1 tbsp soy sauce
- 1 ½ tbsps brown sugar

- 3 ½ tbsps honey
- 1 ½ tbsps chili paste
- ½ tsp salt

Directions:

Add chicken wings in a large bowl and season with onion powder, garlic powder, and salt. Add cornstarch and toss until chicken wings are well coated. Place chicken wings in air fryer basket and air fry at 390 F/ 198 C for 30 minutes. Turn chicken after every 10 minutes. Meanwhile, add all sauce ingredients in a small pan and bring to boil and simmer over low heat for 3-4 minutes. Remove from heat and set aside. Transfer air fried chicken wings in a large bowl. Pour sauce over chicken wings and toss well. Serve and enjoy.

Nutritional Value:

Calories 570, Fat 17.8 g, Carbohydrates 32.3 g

BBQ Chicken Wings

Preparation Time: 10 minutes | Cooking Time: 28 minutes | Serve: 2

Ingredients:

- 6 chicken wings
- ½ tsp garlic powder
- ¼ tsp ginger powder
- 2 tsp soy sauce
- 4 tbsp honey BBQ sauce

Directions:

Preheat the air fryer to 360 F/ 180 C. Place chicken wings in air fryer basket and air fry for 25-28 minutes. Shake basket after every 10 minutes. Meanwhile, in a bowl, mix together honey BBQ sauce, garlic powder, ginger powder, and soy sauce. Add air fried chicken wings in a sauce bowl and toss well to coat. Serve and enjoy.

Nutritional Value:

Calories 422, Fat 19.9 g, Carbohydrates 29.1 g

Lemon Honey Chicken

Preparation Time: 10 minutes | Cooking Time: 15 minutes | Serve: 4

Ingredients:

- 1 egg, lightly beaten
- 1 lb chicken breast, skinless, boneless, and cut into chunks
- 1/3 cup breadcrumbs
- ½ cup cornstarch
- ¼ tsp pepper
- ¾ tsp salt

For sauce:

- 3 tbsps water
- 2 tbsps cornstarch
- ¼ tsp ginger, grated
- 1 tsp garlic powder
- 1 tsp sesame oil
- ½ tbsp lemon zest
- 2 ½ tbsps fresh lemon juice
- 2 tbsps white vinegar
- ¼ cup honey
- 1/3 cup soy sauce

Directions:

Add all sauce ingredients in a saucepan and mix well. Take out 3 tablespoons of sauce mixture from saucepan and add in the large bowl. Set aside saucepan. Add egg in large bowl and mix well with 3 tablespoons of sauce. Add chicken in a bowl and mix well. In a large zip-lock bag, combine breadcrumbs, cornstarch, pepper, and salt. Add chicken and shake well to coat. Preheat the air fryer to 400 F/ 200 C for 8 minutes. Place chicken in air fryer basket and air fry for 8 minutes. Shake basket halfway through. Meanwhile for the sauce: Heat saucepan with sauce over medium-high heat. Stir constantly once the sauce is thickened then turn off the heat. Add air fried chicken in sauce and toss well to coat. Serve and enjoy.

Nutritional Value:

Calories 350, Fat 5.7 g, Carbohydrates 45 g

Korean Chicken Wings

Preparation Time: 10 minutes | Cooking Time: 25 minutes | Serve: 4

Ingredients:

- 2 lbs chicken wings
- ½ tsp pepper

- 1 tsp salt

For sauce:

- 2 tbsps sugar
- 1 tbsp garlic, minced
- 1 tbsp ginger, minced
- 1 tbsp sesame oil

- 1 tsp honey
- 1 tbsp mayonnaise
- 2 tbsps gochujang

Directions:

Preheat the air fryer to 400 F/ 200 C. Season chicken wings with pepper and salt. Add chicken wings into the air fryer basket and air fry for 20 minutes. Turn halfway through. Meanwhile, in a bowl, mix together all sauce ingredients. Add air fried chicken wings to the sauce bowl and toss well. Return chicken wings to the air fryer basket and air fry for 5 minutes more. Serve and enjoy.

Nutritional Value:

Calories 532, Fat 21.5 g, Carbohydrates 14.6 g

Tangy Chicken

Preparation Time: 10 minutes | Cooking Time: 15 minutes | Serve: 4

Ingredients:

- 4 chicken breast, skinless
- 2 tbsps Dijon mustard
- 3 tbsps olive oil
- 2 ½ tbsps soy sauce
- ¼ cup brown sugar
- ¼ cup balsamic vinegar

Directions:

Add all ingredients except chicken in a bowl and mix well. Add chicken and mix until chicken is well coated and let marinate for 30 minutes. Place marinated chicken in air fryer basket and air fry at 380 F/ 193 C for 15 minutes. Serve and enjoy.

Nutritional Value:

Calories 252, Fat 13.3 g, Carbohydrates 10.2 g

Sriracha Chicken Wings

Preparation Time: 10 minutes | Cooking Time: 33 minutes | Serve: 2

Ingredients:

- 1 lb chicken wings
- ½ fresh lime juice
- 1 tbsp butter
- 2 tbsps soy sauce
- 2 tbsps sriracha sauce
- 4 tbsps honey
- 2 tbsps green onion, chopped

Directions:

Preheat the air fryer to 360 F/ 182 C. Add chicken wings to the air fryer basket and air fry for 30 minutes. Turn chicken after every 10 minutes. Meanwhile, add all remaining ingredients except green onion to a small pan and bring to boil for 3 minutes. Once chicken wings are cooked then toss with sauce until well coated. Garnish with green onion and serve.

Nutritional Value:

Calories 361, Fat 16.3 g, Carbohydrates 19.1 g

Asian Meat Recipes

Simple Air Fried Pork Chunks

Preparation Time: 10 minutes | Cooking Time: 12 minutes | Serve: 4

Ingredients:

- 2 eggs
- 2 lbs pork, cut into chunks
- 1 cup cornstarch
- ¼ tsp pepper
- ½ tsp sea salt

Directions:

In a large bowl, mix together cornstarch, pepper, and salt. In another bowl, beat the eggs. Coat pork chunks with cornstarch mixture and dip each chunk into the egg mixture then again coat with cornstarch mixture. Spray air fryer basket from inside with cooking spray. Place pork chunks into the air fryer basket and air fry at 340 F/ 171 C for 10-12 minutes. Serve and enjoy.

Nutritional Value:

Calories 478, Fat 10.2 g, Carbohydrates 29.5 g

Chinese Pork Roast

Preparation Time: 10 minutes | Cooking Time: 16 minutes | Serve: 4

Ingredients:

- 1 lb pork shoulder, cut into slices
- ½ tsp Chinese five spice
- 1 ½ tsps ginger, minced
- ½ tbsp hoisin sauce
- 1 tbsp rice wine
- 1 tbsp sugar

- 1 ½ tsps garlic, minced
- 1 ½ tbsps soy sauce
- 3 tbsps honey

Directions:

Add all ingredients except pork into the microwave-safe bowl and mix well. Add pork slices in a large bowl. Pour half the sauce over the pork slices and mix well and let marinate for half hour. Place marinated pork slices in air fryer basket and air fry at 390 F/ 198 C for 15 minutes. Turn meat halfway through. Meanwhile, microwave half the sauce for 40 seconds. Stir every 10 seconds. Once meat is cooked then brush with sauce and serve.

Nutritional Value:

Calories 408, Fat 24.4 g, Carbohydrates 19.9 g

Spicy Korean Pork

Preparation Time: 10 minutes | Cooking Time: 15 minutes | Serve: 4

Ingredients:

- 1 lb pork shoulder, boneless and cut into slices
- 3 tbsps green onions, sliced
- ½ tbsp sesame seeds
- 2 tbsps chili paste
- 1 tsp sugar
- 1 tbsp rice wine
- 1 tbsp soy sauce
- 1 ½ tbsp ginger garlic paste
- 1 onion, sliced
- 1 tbsp sesame oil

Directions:

In a large bowl, mix together pork, sugar, sesame oil, rice wine, soy sauce, ginger garlic paste, chili paste, and onion and let marinate for 30 minutes. Place marinated pork slices into the air fryer basket and air fry at 400 F/ 200 C for 15 minutes. Turn halfway through. Garnish with sesame seeds and green onion. Serve and enjoy.

Nutritional Value:

Calories 427, Fat 29.9 g, Carbohydrates 10.3 g

Tasty BBQ Beef

Preparation Time: 10 minutes | Cooking Time: 20 minutes | Serve: 4

Ingredients:

- 1 lb flank steak, sliced
- ¼ cup cornstarch

For sauce:

- 1 tbsp water
- 1 tbsp cornstarch
- 1 tsp sesame seeds
- ½ tsp ginger powder
- 1 tbsp chili paste
- 1 garlic clove, minced
- 2 tbsps white vinegar
- ½ cup of soy sauce
- 6 tbsps brown sugar

Directions:

Add sliced steak and cornstarch in a bowl and toss well to coat. Spray air fryer basket from inside with cooking spray. Place steak slices into the air fryer basket and air fry at 390 F/ 198 C for 10 minutes. Turn steak slices to other side and air fry for 10 minutes more. Meanwhile, add all sauce ingredients except water and cornstarch to a saucepan and bring to boil. Turn heat to low and whisk in water and cornstarch. Transfer air fried steak slices to the large mixing bowl and pour sauce over steak. Toss well. Serve and enjoy.

Nutritional Value:

Calories 347, Fat 10.4 g, Carbohydrates 27 g

Crispy Pork Chops

Preparation Time: 10 minutes | Cooking Time: 13 minutes | Serve: 4

Ingredients:

- 6 pork chops, boneless
- 1 ½ cup seasoned breadcrumbs
- 2 egg, lightly beaten
- ¼ cup flour
- ¼ tsp pepper
- ¼ tsp salt

Directions:

Add eggs, breadcrumbs, and flour in three separate shallow bowls. Season pork chops with pepper and salt. Coat pork chops with flour then dip in eggs and coat with breadcrumbs. Place pork chops in air fryer basket and air fry at 360 F/ 182 C for 8 minutes. Turn pork chops to other side and air fry for 5 minutes more. Serve and enjoy.

Nutritional Value:

Calories 609, Fat 37.4 g, Carbohydrates 31.7 g

Ginger Garlic Beef

Preparation Time: 10 minutes | Cooking Time: 25 minutes | Serve: 4

Ingredients:

- 1 lb flank steak, sliced

For sauce:

- ½ cup brown sugar
- ½ cup of water
- ½ cup of soy sauce
- ¼ cup cornstarch

- 1 tbsp garlic, minced
- ½ tsp ginger, minced
- 2 tbsps canola oil

Directions:

Add sliced steak and cornstarch in a large bowl and toss well to coat. Place sliced steak into the air fryer basket and air fry at 390 F/ 198 C for 10 minutes. Turn sliced steak pieces to other side and air fry for 10 minutes more. Meanwhile, add all sauce ingredients in a saucepan and heat over medium-high heat. Cook sauce until begins to low boil. Remove from heat. Once steak is cooked then add in sauce mixture and let it soak for 5 minutes. Remove steak from the sauce and serve.

Nutritional Value:

Calories 402, Fat 16.5 g, Carbohydrates 28.4 g

Spicy Lamb

Preparation Time: 10 minutes | Cooking Time: 10 minutes | Serve: 4

Ingredients:

- 1 lb lamb, cut into ½ inch pieces
- ¼ tsp sugar
- 1 ½ red chili peppers, chopped
- 1 tbsp garlic, minced
- ¾ tbsp soy sauce
- 2 tbsps canola oil
- ½ tsp cayenne
- ½ tbsp cumin powder
- 2 tbsps green onion, chopped
- 1 tsp salt

Directions:

In a large bowl, mix together lamb, cumin powder, cayenne, sugar, red chili peppers, garlic, soy sauce, oil, and salt. Place marinated lamb pieces into the air fryer basket and air fry at 360 F/ 182 C for 10 minutes. Garnish with green onion and serve.

Nutritional Value:

Calories 286, Fat 15.7 g, Carbohydrates 2.3 g

Beef Kabab

Preparation Time: 10 minutes | Cooking Time: 10 minutes | Serve: 4

Ingredients:

- 1 lb beef, cut into chunks
- ½ onion, cut into 1-inch pieces
- 1 bell pepper, cut into 1-inch pieces
- 2 tbsps soy sauce
- 1/3 cup sour cream

Directions:

In a bowl, mix together soy sauce and sour cream. Add beef chunks into the bowl and mix well and let marinate for 30 minutes. Soak wooden skewers in water for 15 minutes. Thread marinated beef chunks, bell peppers, and onions onto skewers. Place prepared skewers in air fryer basket and air fry at 400 F/ 200 C for 10 minutes. Turn halfway through. Serve and enjoy.

Nutritional Value:

Calories 271, Fat 11.2 g, Carbohydrates 5 g

Crispy Grilled Pork

Preparation Time: 10 minutes | Cooking Time: 10 minutes | Serve: 4

Ingredients:

- 1 lb pork shoulder, sliced
- 1 tbsp lemongrass, minced
- ½ tbsp fish sauce
- 1 ½ tsp soy sauce
- 1 tbsp garlic, minced
- 2 tbsps sugar
- 2 tbsps canola oil
- 3 tbsps onion, minced
- 2 tbsps fresh parsley, chopped

Directions:

In a medium bowl, whisk together onions, lemongrass, fish sauce, garlic, oil, soy sauce, and sugar. Add sliced pork into the bowl and mix well and let marinate for 30 minutes. Place marinated pork slices into the air fryer basket and air fry at 400 F/ 200 C for 10 minutes. Turn halfway through. Garnish with fresh parsley and serve.

Nutritional Value:

Calories 425, Fat 31.3 g, Carbohydrates 8 g

Flavorful Lamb Steak

Preparation Time: 10 minutes | Cooking Time: 15 minutes | Serve: 4

Ingredients:

- 1 lb lamb chops, boneless
- 1 tsp cayenne
- ½ tsp cardamom powder
- ¼ tsp ground fennel
- ½ tsp garam masala
- 3 garlic cloves
- 1 tbsp ginger, sliced
- ½ onion, sliced
- 1 tsp salt

Directions:

Add all ingredients except meat into the blender and blend all ingredients for 3-4 minutes. Add meat into the large bowl and pour blended mixture over meat and mix well. Marinate meat for 30 minutes. Place marinated meat into the air fryer basket and air fry at 330 F/ 165 C for 15 minutes. Turn meat halfway through. Serve and enjoy.

Nutritional Value:

Calories 227, Fat 8.5 g, Carbohydrates 3.5 g

Asian Fish & Seafood Recipes

Garlic Lemon Shrimp

Preparation Time: 10 minutes | Cooking Time: 6 minutes | Serve: 4

Ingredients:

- 1 lb shrimp, deveined and peeled
- 1 tbsp fresh lemon juice
- 3 garlic cloves, minced
- ¼ tsp cayenne pepper
- 1 tbsp honey
- 2 tbsps soy sauce
- 2 tbsps olive oil
- ¼ tsp pepper
- ¼ tsp kosher salt

Directions:

Add shrimp into the large bowl. Add remaining ingredients to the shrimp bowl and mix well and let marinate for 15 minutes. Place marinated shrimp into the air fryer basket and air fry at 410 F/ 210 C for 6 minutes. Serve and enjoy.

Nutritional Value:

Calories 220, Fat 9 g, Carbohydrates 7.6 g

Salmon Patties

Preparation Time: 10 minutes | Cooking Time: 8 minutes | Serve: 6

Ingredients:

- 14 oz can salmon, bone removed and drained
- 2 eggs, lightly beaten
- ½ lime zest
- 2 tbsps red curry paste
- ½ cup breadcrumbs
- ¼ tsp salt
- 1 tbsps brown sugar

Directions:

Add all ingredients into the bowl and mix until well combined. Make round patties from mixture and place in air fryer basket. Spray patties with cooking spray. Air fry patties at 360 F/ 182 C for 4 minutes then turns to other side and air fry for 4 minutes more. Serve and enjoy.

Nutritional Value:

Calories 174, Fat 7.4 g, Carbohydrates 9.1 g

Shrimp with Sauce

Preparation Time: 10 minutes | Cooking Time: 9 minutes | Serve: 4

Ingredients:

- 1 egg
- 1 tbsp fresh parsley, chopped
- ½ lb shrimp, peeled and deveined

- ½ cup breadcrumbs
- 2 tbsps cornstarch
- ¼ tsp salt

For sauce:

- 1 tsp sesame oil
- ½ tsp paprika
- ½ tbsp brown sugar
- 1 tbsp white vinegar

- ½ tbsp chili sauce
- 1 garlic clove, minced
- 1 tbsp butter, melted
- ½ cup mayonnaise

Directions:

Add all sauce ingredients in a small bowl and mix well and set aside. Add eggs, breadcrumbs, and cornstarch in three separate shallow dishes. Coat shrimp with cornstarch then dip in egg mixture and finally coat with breadcrumbs. Place parchment paper piece in air fryer basket. Place shrimp on parchment paper and air fry at 350 F/ 176 C for 4 minutes. Turn shrimp to other side and air fry for 4-5 minutes more. Garnish with parsley and serve with sauce.

Nutritional Value:

Calories 309, Fat 16.6 g, Carbohydrates 23 g

Honey Soy Salmon

Preparation Time: 10 minutes | Cooking Time: 12 minutes | Serve: 2

Ingredients:

- 2 salmon fillets, skin on
- ¾ tbsp soy sauce
- 3 tbsps sriracha
- 6 tbsps honey

Directions:

In a bowl, mix together soy sauce, sriracha, and honey. Add salmon fillets to the bowl and coat well with the sauce and let marinate for 30 minutes. Spray air fryer basket from inside with cooking spray. Place marinated salmon in air fryer basket and air fry at 400 F/ 200 C for 12 minutes. Serve and enjoy.

Nutritional Value:

Calories 453, Fat 11 g, Carbohydrates 56.9 g

Tasty Asian Shrimp

Preparation Time: 10 minutes | Cooking Time: 10 minutes | Serve: 4

Ingredients:

- 1 lb shrimp, peeled and deveined
- ¼ tsp ginger, minced
- 2 garlic cloves, minced
- 2 ½ tbsps soy sauce
- 2 ½ tbsps chili sauce
- 1 tbsp cornstarch

Directions:

Spray air fryer basket from inside with cooking spray. Coat shrimp with cornstarch and place into the air fryer basket. Air fry shrimp at 350 F/ 176 C for 5 minutes. Turn shrimp to other side and spray with cooking spray and air fry for 5 minutes more. Meanwhile, for the sauce in a bowl, mix together remaining ingredients. Add air fried shrimp in a sauce bowl and toss well. Serve and enjoy.

Nutritional Value:

Calories 151, Fat 2 g, Carbohydrates 5.1 g

Healthy Salmon Patties

Preparation Time: 10 minutes | Cooking Time: 7 minutes | Serve: 2

Ingredients:

- 1 egg, lightly beaten
- 8 oz fresh salmon fillet, mince
- ½ tsp garlic powder
- 2 tbsps fresh parsley, chopped
- 1/8 tsp salt

Directions:

Preheat the air fryer to 390 F/ 198 C for 5 minutes. Add all ingredients into the bowl and mix well to combine. Make patties from mixture and place in air fryer basket. Air fry patties in preheated air fryer for 7 minutes. Serve and enjoy.

Nutritional Value:

Calories 184, Fat 9.2 g, Carbohydrates 0.7 g

Sriracha Salmon

Preparation Time: 10 minutes | Cooking Time: 14 minutes | Serve: 2

Ingredients:

- 2 salmon fillets
- ½ tbsp soy sauce
- 1 ½ tbsp sriracha
- 1 ½ tbsp white vinegar
- 1/3 cup ketchup
- 1/3 cup bourbon
- 6 tbsps brown sugar

Directions:

In a saucepan, combine together brown sugar, soy sauce, sriracha, vinegar, ketchup, and bourbon. Bring to boil. Turn heat to low and simmer for 8 minutes. Brush salmon fillet with sauce and place in air fryer basket. Air fry salmon at 400 F/ 200 C for 14 minutes. Serve with sauce and enjoy.

Nutritional Value:

Calories 478, Fat 11.1 g, Carbohydrates 39.2 g

Ginger Garlic Shrimp

Preparation Time: 10 minutes | Cooking Time: 10 minutes | Serve: 4

Ingredients:

- 1 lb shrimp, peeled and deveined
- 1/8 tsp ginger, minced
- 2 garlic cloves, minced
- 2 tbsps soy sauce
- 1 tbsp green onion, sliced
- 2 tbsps Thai chili sauce
- 1 tbsp cornstarch
- 1 tsp sesame seeds

Directions:

Spray air fryer basket with cooking spray. Toss shrimp with cornstarch and place into the air fryer basket. Air fry shrimp at 350 F/ 176 C for 5 minutes. Shake basket well and cook for 5 minutes more. Meanwhile, in a bowl, mix together soy sauce, ginger, garlic, and chili sauce. Add shrimp to the bowl and mix well. Sprinkle with green onions and sesame seeds. Serve and enjoy.

Nutritional Value:

Calories 164, Fat 2.3 g, Carbohydrates 7.5 g

Lemon Chili Shrimp

Preparation Time: 10 minutes | Cooking Time: 7 minutes | Serve: 4

Ingredients:

- 1 lb shrimp, peeled and deveined
- 1 tbsp canola oil
- 1 lemon, sliced
- 1 red chili, sliced
- 1/2 tsp garlic powder
- Pepper
- Salt

Directions:

Preheat the air fryer to 400 F/ 200 C. Spray air fryer basket with cooking spray. Add all ingredients into the mixing bowl and toss well. Transfer shrimp mixture into the air fryer basket and air fry for 5 minutes. Shake basket well and cook for 2 minutes more. Serve and enjoy.

Nutritional Value:

Calories 167, Fat 5.4 g, Carbohydrates 2 g

Crispy Coconut Shrimp

Preparation Time: 10 minutes | Cooking Time: 5 minutes | Serve: 4

Ingredients:

- 16 oz shrimp, peeled
- 2 egg whites
- 1/4 tsp cayenne pepper
- 1/2 cup shredded coconut
- 1/2 cup breadcrumbs
- 1/2 tsp salt

Directions:

Preheat the air fryer at 400 F/ 200 C. Spray air fryer basket with cooking spray. Whisk egg whites in a shallow dish. In a bowl, mix together shredded coconut, breadcrumbs, and cayenne pepper. Dip shrimp into the egg mixture then coat with coconut mixture and place into the air fryer basket. Air fry at 400 F/ 200 C for 5 minutes. Serve and enjoy.

Nutritional Value:

Calories 232, Fat 6 g, Carbohydrates 13.1 g

Asian Side Dishes

Sweet Potato Bites

Preparation Time: 10 minutes | Cooking Time: 15 minutes | Serve: 2

Ingredients:

- 2 sweet potato, diced into 1-inch cubes
- 1 tsp red chili flakes
- 1/2 cup fresh parsley, chopped
- 1 1/2 tsps cinnamon
- 2 tbsps canola oil
- 2 tbsps honey

Directions:

Preheat air fryer at 350 F/ 176 C. Add all ingredients into the bowl and toss well. Place sweet potato mixture into the air fryer basket. Cook in preheated air fryer for 15 minutes. Serve and enjoy.

Nutritional Value:

Calories 300, Fat 14.3 g, Carbohydrates 43.2 g

Crispy Cauliflower Florets

Preparation Time: 10 minutes | Cooking Time: 20 minutes | Serve: 2

Ingredients:

- 2 cups cauliflower florets, boiled
- 1 egg, beaten
- 1 tbsp canola oil
- 1/4 cup flour
- 1/2 cup breadcrumbs
- 1/2 tsp garlic powder
- 1/2 tsp chili powder
- 1/2 tbsp mix herb
- 2 tbsps parmesan cheese, grated
- Salt

Directions:

In a bowl, combine together breadcrumbs, garlic powder, chili powder, mix herb, salt, and cheese. Add oil in breadcrumbs mixture and mix well. Add flour in shallow dish and beaten egg in small bowl. Dip cauliflower floret in beaten egg then in flour and finally coat with breadcrumbs. Preheat the air fryer at 350 F/ 176 C. Place coated cauliflower florets in air fryer basket and air fry for 20 minutes. Shake basket halfway through. Serve and enjoy.

Nutritional Value:

Calories 286, Fat 11 g, Carbohydrates 37.7 g

Banana Chips

Preparation Time: 10 minutes | Cooking Time: 15 minutes | Serve: 3

Ingredients:

- 2 large raw bananas, peel and sliced
- 1 tsp canola oil
- 1/4 tsp turmeric powder
- 1/2 tsp red chili powder
- 1 tsp salt

Directions:

In a bowl add water, turmeric powder, and salt. Stir well. Add sliced bananas in bowl water soak for 10 minutes. Drain well and dry chips with a paper towel. Preheat the air fryer to 350 F/ 176 C. Add banana slices in mixing bowl and toss with oil, chili powder, and salt. Place banana slices in air fryer basket and air fry for 15 minutes. Shake basket halfway through. Serve and enjoy.

Nutritional Value:

Calories 96, Fat 2 g, Carbohydrates 21.1 g

Broccoli with Pine Nuts

Preparation Time: 10 minutes | Cooking Time: 15 minutes | Serve: 6

Ingredients:

- 1 lb broccoli florets
- 1 tbsp garlic, minced
- 1 1/2 tbsps canola oil
- 1 fresh lime juice
- 1/4 cup pine nuts

- 1 tsp rice vinegar
- 2 tsps sriracha
- 2 tbsps soy sauce
- Salt

Directions:

In a bowl, toss together broccoli, oil, salt, and garlic. Add broccoli into the air fryer basket and air fry at 400 F/ 200 C for 15 minutes. Shake basket halfway through. Meanwhile, in a microwave safe bowl, mix together rice vinegar, sriracha, and soy sauce and microwave for 10 seconds. Transfer air fried broccoli into the large bowl. Pour vinegar mixture over the broccoli and toss well. Add lime juice and pine nuts and toss well. Serve and enjoy.

Nutritional Value:

Calories 102, Fat 7.6 g, Carbohydrates 7 g

Garlic Cauliflower Florets

Preparation Time: 10 minutes | Cooking Time: 20 minutes | Serve: 4

Ingredients:

- 5 cups cauliflower florets
- 6 garlic cloves, chopped
- 1/2 tsp cumin powder

- 4 tablespoons canola oil
- 1/2 tsp coriander powder
- 1/2 tsp salt

Directions:

Add all ingredients into the large bowl and toss well. Add cauliflower florets into the air fryer basket and air fry at 400 F/ 200 C for 20 minutes. Shake basket halfway through. Serve and enjoy.

Nutritional Value:

Calories 163, Fat 14.2 g, Carbohydrates 8.2 g

Asian Vegetable & Tofu Recipes

Roasted Broccoli with Peanuts

Preparation Time: 10 minutes | Cooking Time: 20 minutes | Serve: 4

Ingredients:

- 1 lb broccoli, cut into florets
- 1/3 cup peanuts, roasted
- 1 tsp white vinegar
- 2 tsps sriracha
- 2 tsps honey
- 2 tbsps soy sauce
- 1 tbsp garlic, minced
- 1 ½ tbsps canola oil
- Salt

Directions:

In a large mixing bowl, toss broccoli with garlic, oil, and salt. Add broccoli into the air fryer basket and air fry at 400 F/ 200 C for 15-20 minutes. Shake basket halfway through. Meanwhile, in a microwave-safe bowl, mix together honey, vinegar, sriracha, and soy sauce and microwave for 10-15 seconds. Transfer air fried broccoli to the large bowl. Add peanuts and honey mixture over broccoli and toss well. Serve and enjoy.

Nutritional Value:

Calories 175, Fat 11.6 g, Carbohydrates 14.2 g

Garlic Brussels sprouts

Preparation Time: 10 minutes | Cooking Time: 8 minutes | Serve: 4

Ingredients:

- 1 lb Brussels sprouts, clean and trimmed
- 2 tsps canola oil
- 4 garlic cloves, minced
- 1 tsp dried parsley
- ¼ tsp salt

Directions:

Add all ingredients into the large bowl and toss well. Pour Brussels sprouts mixture into the air fryer basket and air fry at 390 F/ 198 C for 8 minutes. Serve and enjoy.

Nutritional Value:

Calories 74, Fat 2.7 g, Carbohydrates 11.3 g

Delicious Air Fried Tofu

Preparation Time: 10 minutes | Cooking Time: 20 minutes | Serve: 4

Ingredients:

- 1 block firm tofu, cut into 1-inch cubes
- 1 tbsp cornstarch
- 2 tsps sesame oil
- 1 tsp white vinegar
- 2 tbsps soy sauce

Directions:

Add tofu, sesame oil, vinegar, and soy sauce in a large bowl and let it marinate for 15 minutes. Toss marinated tofu with cornstarch and place in air fryer basket. Air fry tofu at 370 F/ 187 C for 20 minutes. Shake basket halfway through. Serve and enjoy.

Nutritional Value:

Calories 48, Fat 3.2 g, Carbohydrates 2.8 g

Lemon Garlic Broccoli Florets

Preparation Time: 10 minutes | Cooking Time: 13 minutes | Serve: 4

Ingredients:

- 1 lb broccoli, cut into florets
- 1 tbsp fresh lemon juice
- 3 garlic cloves, minced
- 1 tbsp olive oil
- 1 tbsp sesame seeds

Directions:

Add all ingredients into the bowl and toss well. Add broccoli into the air fryer basket and air fry at 400 F/ 200 C for 13 minutes. Serve and enjoy.

Nutritional Value:

Calories 86, Fat 5 g, Carbohydrates 8.9 g

Crispy Tofu

Preparation Time: 10 minutes | Cooking Time: 8 minutes | Serve: 4

Ingredients:

- 15 oz firm tofu, drain and cut into cubes
- 3/4 cup cornstarch
- 1/4 cup cornmeal
- 1 tsp chili flakes
- Pepper
- Salt

Directions:

In a bowl, mix together cornmeal, cornstarch, chili flakes, pepper, and salt. Add tofu cubes in cornmeal mixture and coat well. Preheat air fryer at 350 F/ 176 C. Spray air fryer basket with cooking spray. Place coated tofu in air fryer basket and air fry for 8 minutes. Shake basket halfway through. Serve with enjoy.

Nutritional Value:

- Calories 194
- Fat 4.7 g
- Carbohydrates 29.6 g

Asian Dessert Recipes

Delicious Chinese Doughnuts

Preparation Time: 10 minutes | Cooking Time: 8 minutes | Serve: 8

Ingredients:

- 2 cups all-purpose flour
- ¾ cup of coconut milk
- 6 tbsps coconut oil
- 1 tbsp baking powder
- 2 tsps sugar
- ½ tsp sea salt

Directions:

Preheat the air fryer to 350 F/ 176 C. In a bowl, mix together flour, baking powder, sugar, and salt. Add coconut oil and mix well. Add coconut milk and mix until well combined. Knead dough for 3-4 minutes. Roll dough half inch thick and using cookie cutter cut doughnuts. Place doughnuts in cake pan and brush with oil. Place cake pan in air fryer basket and air fry doughnuts for 5 minutes. Turn doughnuts to other side and air fry for 3 minutes more. Serve and enjoy.

Nutritional Value:

Calories 259, Fat 15.9 g, Carbohydrates 27 g

Sweet & Crisp Bananas

Preparation Time: 10 minutes | Cooking Time: 10 minutes | Serve: 4

Ingredients:

- 4 ripe bananas, peeled and cut in half pieces
- 1 tbsp cashew, crushed
- 1/2 cup breadcrumbs

- 1 egg, beaten
- 1 1/2 tbsps Coconut Oil
- 1 tbsp almond meal
- 1/4 cup corn flour
- 1 1/2 tbsps cinnamon sugar

Directions:

Heat coconut oil in a pan over medium heat and add breadcrumbs in the pan and stir for 3-4 minutes. Remove pan from heat and transfer breadcrumbs in a bowl. Add almond meal and crush cashew in breadcrumbs and mix well. Dip banana half in corn flour then in egg and finally coat with breadcrumbs. Place coated banana in air fryer basket. Sprinkle with Cinnamon Sugar. Air fry at 350 F/ 176 C for 10 minutes. Serve and enjoy.

Nutritional Value:

Calories 282, Fat 9 g, Carbohydrates 46 g

Banana Muffins

Preparation Time: 10 minutes | Cooking Time: 10 minutes | Serve: 2

Ingredients:

- 1/4 cup banana, mashed
- 1/4 cup oats
- 1 tbsp walnuts, chopped
- 1/4 cup flour
- 1/2 tsp baking powder
- 1/4 cup powdered sugar
- 1/4 cup butter

Directions:

Spray four muffin molds with cooking spray and set aside. In a bowl, mix together mashed banana, walnuts, sugar, and butter. In another bowl, mix together flour, baking powder, and oats. Add flour mixture to the banana mixture and mix well. Pour batter into the prepared muffin mold. Place in air fryer basket and cook at 320 F/ 160 C for 10 minutes. Remove muffins from air fryer and allow to cool completely. Serve and enjoy.

Nutritional Value:

Calories 192, Fat 12.3 g, Carbohydrates 19.4 g

Easy Blueberry Muffins

Preparation Time: 10 minutes | Cooking Time: 14 minutes | Serve: 2

Ingredients:

- 1 egg
- 3/4 cup blueberries
- 2 tbsps sugar
- 1 tsp baking powder
- 2/3 cup flour
- 3 tbsps butter, melted
- 1/3 cup milk

Directions:

Spray four silicone muffins cups with cooking spray and set aside. In a bowl, mix together all ingredients until well combined. Pour batter into the prepared muffins cups. Place muffin cups in air fryer basket and cook at 320 F/ 160 C for 14 minutes. Serve and enjoy.

Nutritional Value:

Calories 435, Fat 20.9 g, Carbohydrates 55 g

Spicy Mix Nuts

Preparation Time: 5 minutes | Cooking Time: 4 minutes | Serve: 6

Ingredients:

- 2 cup mix nuts
- 1 tbsp butter, melted
- 1 tsp chili powder
- 1 tsp ground cumin
- 1 tsp pepper
- 1 tsp salt

Directions:

Add all ingredients in a mixing bowl and toss until well coated. Preheat the air fryer at 350 F/ 176 C for 5 minutes. Add mix nuts in air fryer basket and air fry for 4 minutes. Shake basket halfway through. Serve and enjoy.

Nutritional Value:

Calories 316, Fat 29 g, Carbohydrates 11.3 g

Asian Keto Recipes

Healthy Air Fried Okra

Preparation Time: 10 minutes | Cooking Time: 15 minutes | Serve: 2

Ingredients:

- ½ lb okra, trimmed and sliced
- 1 tsp vegetable oil
- ¼ tsp chili powder
- ¼ tsp garlic powder
- 1/8 tsp pepper
- ¼ tsp salt

Directions:

Preheat the air fryer to 350 F/ 176 C. Add all ingredients into the mixing bowl and toss well. Transfer okra into the air fryer basket and air fry for 10 minutes. Shake basket halfway through. Toss again and cook for 2 minutes more. Serve and enjoy.

Nutritional Value:

Calories 68, Fat 2.6 g, Carbohydrates 9 g

Sausage Meatballs

Preparation Time: 10 minutes | Cooking Time: 15 minutes | Serve: 4

Ingredients:

- 3.5 oz sausage meat
- 3 tbsps almond flour
- 1 tsp ginger garlic paste
- 1/2 onion, diced
- Pepper
- Salt

Directions:

Preheat the air fryer to 360 F/ 182 C. Spray air fryer basket with cooking spray. Add all ingredients into the mixing bowl and mix until well combined. Make small balls from mixture and place into the air fryer basket and air fry for 15 minutes. Serve and enjoy.

Nutritional Value:

Calories 126, Fat 9.9 g, Carbohydrates 3.2 g

Chicken Meatballs

Preparation Time: 10 minutes | Cooking Time: 10 minutes | Serve: 4

Ingredients:

- 1 lb ground chicken
- 1 tbsp soy sauce
- 1 tbsp hoisin sauce
- 1/2 cup fresh cilantro, chopped
- 1/4 cup shredded coconut
- 1 tsp sesame oil
- 1 tsp sriracha
- 2 green onions, chopped
- Pepper
- Salt

Directions:

Spray air fryer basket with cooking spray. Add all ingredients into the large mixing bowl and mix until well combined. Make small balls from mixture and place into the air fryer basket. Air fry at 350 F/ 176 C for 10 minutes. Turn halfway through. Serve and enjoy.

Nutritional Value:

Calories 258, Fat 11.4 g, Carbohydrates 3.7 g

Delicious Chicken Kebabs

Preparation Time: 10 minutes | Cooking Time: 6 minutes | Serve: 3

Ingredients:

- 1 lb chicken mince
- 1/4 tsp turmeric powder
- 1 egg, lightly beaten
- 1/3 cup fresh parsley, chopped
- 2 garlic cloves
- 4 oz onion, chopped
- 1/2 tsp black pepper
- 1 tbsp fresh lemon juice
- 1/4 cup almond flour
- 2 green onion, chopped

Directions:

Add all ingredients into the food processor and process until well combined. Transfer chicken mixture to the bowl and place in the fridge for 30 minutes. Divide mixture into the six equal portions and roll around the soaked wooden skewers. Spray air fryer basket with cooking spray. Place kebab skewers into the air fryer basket and air fry at 400 F/200 C for 6 minutes. Serve and enjoy.

Nutritional Value:

Calories 329, Fat 10.9 g, Carbohydrates 7.9 g

Easy Chinese Chicken Wings

Preparation Time: 5 minutes | Cooking Time: 30 minutes | Serve: 2

Ingredients:

- 4 chicken wings
- 1 tsp mixed spice
- 1 tbsp soy sauce
- 1 tbsp Chinese spice
- Pepper
- Salt

Directions:

Add chicken wings into the bowl. Add remaining ingredients and toss well. Transfer chicken wings into the air fryer basket. Air fry at 350 F/ 176 C for 15 minutes. Turn chicken to other side and cook for 15 minutes more. Serve and enjoy.

Nutritional Value:

Calories 260, Fat 18.3 g, Carbohydrates 0.5 g

Conclusion

We hope you enjoyed the book on "Air Fryer Cookbook 250".

Air fryers are easy to operate and can be used by just about anyone. The fryer is designed to cook food at a faster pace, thereby saving time, while keeping the flavor of the dish.

Printed in Great Britain
by Amazon